"THIS BOOK WAS WRITTEN FOR
ORDINARY PEOPLE . . ."

those with jobs and families and responsibilities; those who have no rich relatives or other sources of timely windfalls; those who have dreamed of owning a weekend hideaway, a part-time farm, a permanent country home, or a pleasant, peaceful place to retire—and have, or hope to have, a moderate sum saved against the day when it is possible to "get out into the country" . . .

"FLY FROM THE CITY IF YOU WANT . . . **BUYING COUNTRY PROPERTY** SHOULD EASE THE TRIP!"

—Organic Gardening and Farming

BUYING COUNTRY PROPERTY

Herbert R. Moral

A NATIONAL GENERAL COMPANY

This low-priced Bantam Book has been completely reset in a type face designed for easy reading, and was printed from new plates. It contains the complete text of the original hard-cover edition.
NOT ONE WORD HAS BEEN OMITTED.

BUYING COUNTRY PROPERTY
A Bantam Book / published by arrangement with Garden Way Publishing Co.

PRINTING HISTORY
Significant portions of this book, together with the illustrations, first appeared in the book *Buying Country Property*, published by Ed Robinson's "Have-More" Plan in 1947.
Garden Way Publishing Co. edition published January 1972
Bantam edition published November 1972
2nd printing

Published simultaneously in the United States and Canada

Bantam Books are published by Bantam Books, Inc., a National General company. Its trade-mark, consisting of the words "Bantam Books" and the portrayal of a bantam, is registered in the United States Patent Office and in other countries. Marca Registrada. Bantam Books, Inc., 666 Fifth Avenue, New York, N.Y. 10019.

PRINTED IN THE UNITED STATES OF AMERICA

CONTENTS

Chapter		Page
One	DO YOU KNOW WHAT YOU WANT?	1
Two	HOW TO DECIDE WHAT YOU CAN AFFORD	19
Three	HOW TO GET THE MOST OUT OF REAL ESTATE MEN	41
Four	FACTS TO REMEMBER ABOUT LAND	57
Five	HOW TO JUDGE THE TRUE CONDITION OF A HOUSE	81
Six	WHEN IS IT WORTH WHILE TO REMODEL?	107
Seven	HOW TO GET THE MOST MORTGAGE FOR THE LEAST MONEY	125
Eight	CHECK THESE TWENTY-FIVE SOURCES OF TROUBLE BEFORE BUYING	145

Buying Country Property

PREFACE

You've decided to buy a piece of country property; you know just what you want—a secret country weekend hideaway, a part-time farm, a permanent country home, a future retirement home. How do you move from your exciting plans to the reality of ownership? Who do you turn to for expert, unbiased assistance? How do you avoid the pitfalls awaiting the unwary buyer?

We asked ourselves these same questions, and then wrote this book to help the buyer through the complete transaction of finding the appropriate property to signing the papers at the closing. We have included advice on working with realtors, evaluating the possible productivity of your land, estimating the true condition of the home. After reading this book, you will be better able to cope with decisions about whether to remodel or build anew, and you will be aided in deciding just how much you can invest.

Individuals decide to buy country property for varying purposes. Within the context of this book, we have given advice which all prospective buyers will find helpful. There is specific information for those who hope to grow family food on their property or do part-time farming; there are also specific considerations for the country weekender. It is our belief that the more aware you are of the different types of country living, the more likely you are to buy property which meets your specifications.

Of course, the final decision in your purchase still rests with you, the buyer. There will be many pressures from people who stand to gain from your decision. If *Buying Country Property* is used correctly, it will be the unbiased friend you turn to for guidance and reassurance.

It is our hope that before you complete the major business transactions of buying property, you will be aware of the true condition of the homestead you are considering. Your care and concern before you buy will be rewarded in the pleasure you gain from owning country property which suits your needs.

Chapter One

DO YOU KNOW WHAT YOU WANT?

It is a curious fact that most families embark on the most important financial transaction of an average lifetime without any knowledge of what they are getting into; in fact, with a deplorable unawareness that there are a lot of things they really ought to know.

That transaction, of course, is the buying of property for a home and, for the purposes of this book, that means country or semi-rural suburban property. In the important financial phase of country living there has been what almost seems like a conspiracy of silence. The family which has decided on what Ralph Borsodi so aptly calls the "flight from the city" will get precious little help from the sources that might be expected to want the family to make a go of things.

There are hundreds of articles on house-planning with pictures of enchanting dream houses, charming interiors, ingenious floor plans and lovely landscaping. Prices of these houses are mentioned reluctantly and tentatively—if at all. The reader may be told he may get a mortgage if he hasn't the cash, but the grimmer aspects of choosing, buying and financing the home are resolutely shunned.

Then there are those "back-to-the-land" chronicles, the sagas of people who have found an earthly heaven at Green Acres up in Vermont, or a soil-and-climate paradise in lower California. As these narratives unfold we learn that Aunt Hattie had left the author her quaint old shack on the outskirts of Brattleboro; or that this is the acre of land he bought fifteen years ago; or that he received a rather satisfactory check for the moving picture rights to a short story. One gets the feeling that it was all a lark—an interlude made more pleasant by the thought that here was material for a book and ahead lay the return to Greenwich Village or Nob Hill.

It is true there is a wide choice of specific and excellent books written for those who plan commercial farms. And because farming is a business as well as a way of life, these books usually are complete and accurate in their treatment of the buying of farm property.

This book, however, is written for ordinary people—those who have jobs and families and responsibilities; for those who have no rich relatives or other sources of timely windfalls. It is written for those who have or hope to have a moderate sum saved against the day when it is possible to "get out into the country." It is aimed at the family convinced that the Garden Way of Living is the answer to the many problems that plague the cities and suburbs today; it is aimed at the individual who would like to savor weekends in the country, away from the hustle and bustle of his weekday life.

There is much hope and promise for the land-hungry city-dweller in these experiences. There is plenty of evidence from other sources that despite their lack of foreknowledge, people who really *want* to enjoy country living somehow or other attain that goal. A study made by the New York State Agricultural Extension Service at Cornell University of a group of families that had moved from the city to smaller localities, disclosed that although many of the families were dissatisfied with one or more aspects of their transition, almost 95 per cent gave positive assurance that they preferred to remain in the country. This reveals that the country does offer a rewarding way of life. The rewards can be greater if the approach is made with a moderate amount of forethought.

It may occur to you that there are people whose business it is to help you buy country property—the real estate broker, the architect, the builder, the banker. This is true, though unfortunately with reservation. These people want you satisfied and happy, but, with the exception of the banker, theirs is a rather short-term concern with your welfare. Generally speaking, the owner of the property is interested only until he pockets his price. The real estate broker, to a large extent, is interested only until he draws his commission. The architect and the builder, while they want your good-will, are off to other operations while you are left to your own devices in the houses they have planned and built.

Banks or lending institutions are committed to your welfare for the period of time in which your mortgage is outstanding. They will probably offer you the most constructive help as far as your actual financing is concerned. But they, too, have an interest to serve that may not always coincide exactly with yours.

YOU ARE THE FINAL ARBITER

Buying country property, if it is to be a satisfying experience, demands, among other things, a knowledge on your part of how to choose and deal with those others who must necessarily enter into the transaction with you. Unless you pay cash for your property, it will actually be up to you to determine the reasonable limits to which it would be practical for you to buy and borrow. It will to a large extent be up to you as to what to sign, and whether to sign, at that unnerving point when the inevitable flood of papers descends upon you. It will be up to you to check your own natural enthusiasm against the judgment of those who are in a position to offer authoritative and objective advice. It will help you to correlate the opinions of architects, builders, real estate brokers and bankers, but these will have to be weighed against a full realization of your own rights, and a realistic cognizance of your resources, and the maximum extent of responsibilities that you will be able to assume.

This, then, is why this book on country property has been written. It won't make you an "expert" in the many fields which it covers, but it will attempt to steer you around the shoals and reefs which may lurk between you and a sound property investment.

As you may have gathered, this book is not written primarily for the person interested in suburban or "development" property. With that class of property, your opportunities for thought and judgment will be limited. Not only are the homes basically similar, but financing plans, too, are pretty much standardized. You take your choice of a Cape Cod Colonial, an English Tudor, or a Spanish Mediterranean villa (probably jerry-built) all with the same postage stamp lawns and tiny back yards. Rather, this book is directed at those who have an interest in the *real* country; who want to buy property as far out in the real country as their work and finances will permit. It is to help those who *do* believe in "a little land, a lot of living"; who want to use their land productively; who enjoy the pleasure as well as the profit of having living things around them.

WHAT SORT OF PLACE DO YOU WANT?

The secret of buying country property successfully lies primarily in knowing what you want. Once you know exactly what kind of place you want, and how much you want to spend, the battle is far from over, but you're on the road to victory.

If you do happen to have a clear picture of your needs and limitations, consider yourself an exception to the rule. Real estate agents are quite accustomed to the indecision of their prospects. If you explain carefully that you want, say twelve acres of good land with a small house and barn, you may be sure the broker will lead you to a big house on three acres of stony hillside with a beautiful view. And, if you object, he will say: "But it does have a wonderful view. Most people want a good view!" The real estate broker has learned from much experience that the majority of city people wind up buying something quite different from what they said they wanted.

Farmers are different. Farmers usually buy just what they want. In fact, it is surprising how little difficulty a farmer has in choosing a new farm. Often he located the place by mail! The reason is simply that a farmer knows exactly how many acres he needs for tillage and pasture, and the size of the hay loft he will require—even the number of stanchions he will need. The dairy farmer planning to wholesale milk knows that he will have to keep about eighteen milking cows to make a living. With dry stock he must have sufficient crop land to raise thirty-six tons of corn, oats and wheat, and a hundred tons of hay. He will require sixty acres of pasture, a milk room, milk cooler, tractor, etc. The farmer who knows what he wants is a true farmer. The "gentleman farmer" is a different breed of farmer entirely.

Knowing what he wants, the true farmer doesn't need help from anybody in buying country property except perhaps the banker. But the story is different with the rest of us.

Let us consider the six fundamental ways a man can live in the country:

(1) He can work in the city and own a country home.
(2) He can operate a part-time farm.
(3) He can work a full-time farm.
(4) He can have a business or profession in his home in the country.
(5) He can retire to a home in the country.

(6) He can own a second home in the country for leisure living.

Now, if you can decide the category into which you fit, you can go about looking for a suitable place. Unfortunately, most people want to combine two or more methods of living in the country. That complicates matters greatly.

The first step necessary in making up your mind, and your wife's mind, too, is to give some thought to the six types of places we have listed.

A COUNTRY HOME FOR A CITY WORKER

Your principal source of income with this type of place will obviously be your job in town. So, the property you choose must be close enough to your work and transportation so that you can commute back and forth each day.

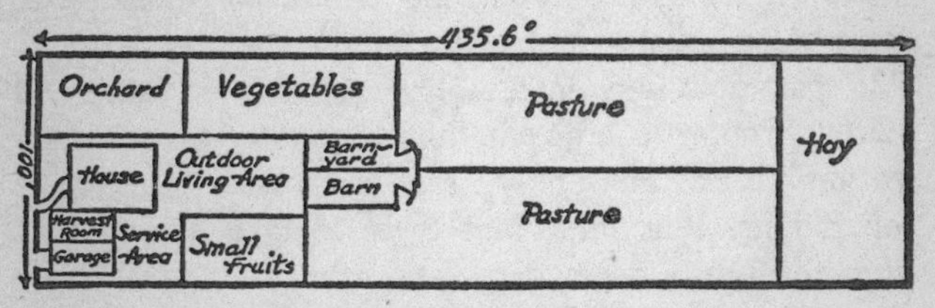

A suggested layout for a homestead, designed to make the most efficient use of an acre of ground, long and narrow in shape.

An hour's time each way is more than you would want to spend in travel. This would mean that you would be away from home more than ten hours a day for at least five days a week. This definitely limits the amount of "living" you can do on your country place.

It has been estimated that the average city commuter, after apportioning the usual time for his necessary daily functions and activities, including relaxation, has approximately twenty hours of time left a week. It is surprising how much you can accomplish by devoting twenty hours a week to your place in the country. *Once you get your place set up and running,* and with proper organization, a large garden, fruit trees, berries, and chickens can be handled, in an hour or so of spare time a day—with a large percentage of the family's food provided. If that is your goal, you must keep it in mind as you search for your place.

A PART-TIME FARM

Often a family buys a country home, and after acquiring some experience, they expand into a part-time farm. This means raising and selling one or more cash crops. The part-time farm invariably requires more land, and certainly more equipment than a country home where raising part of the family's food is the sum total of the operations. It is important then, to take a long look into the future when deciding on your country home. Often forethought will make your transition to a part-time farm from a family food operation very smooth.

THE COMMERCIAL FARM

As we have previously pointed out in some detail, the true farmer rarely has trouble choosing a farm. His mind is pretty well made up as to just the type of farm he wants. He has only the time-consuming business of finding the right farm, and there are many official agencies ready to give him help.

The "gentleman farmer," the man with plenty of money to make a farm a hobby, generally buys his farm from the standpoint of a place to live, or for some other personal reason. At any rate he can afford to put enough money into his farm to transform it into just what he wants. In short, buying country property ceases to be a problem when a man has plenty of money.

The city man who is interested in buying a commercial farm with his hard-earned savings, and hopes to make it pay by farming it himself, is the man who has the most obstacles to overcome in buying country property, is the man who needs the most help, and unfortunately, is also the man who is least likely to succeed.

Frankly, the city man who wants to learn the intricacies of buying a commercial farm won't be helped much by this book, *"unless he has already learned enough about commercial farming to know the kind of farm he wants to work."* Before he is in a position to make this decision, he may have to read a number of books on various kinds of commercial farming. And then, if he is especially prudent, he will work on a successful farm of the type he some day wants to own

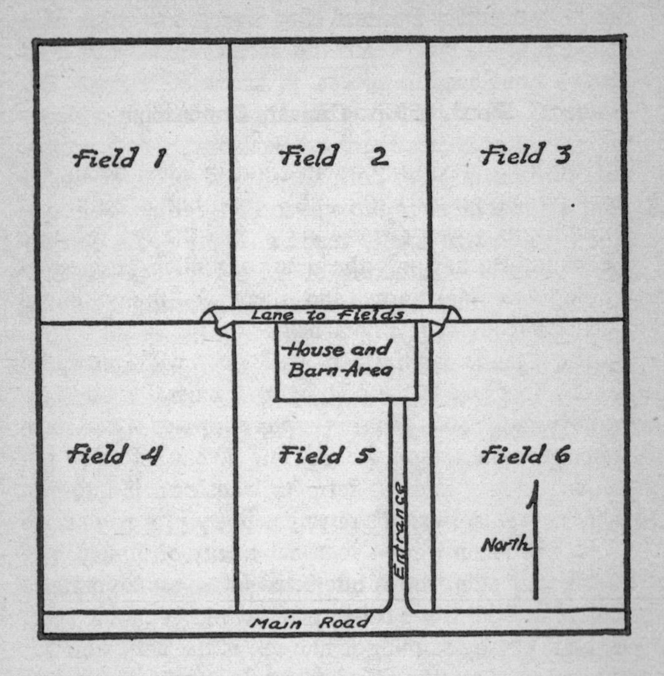

For a commercial farm, location of the house and other buildings at the center affords the maximum efficiency. If a side of the farm is ½ mile long, the farthest point in a field is little more than ¼ mile from the house or barn.

himself. He might also, if he happens to be fortunately enough situated from a financial standpoint, buy a farm of the type he wants and start farming part-time to get his experience, while at the same time holding on to his regular job.

No city man should invest all his money in buying a commercial farm before he feels confident of his ability to operate it successfully. Commercial farming is a far more complex business than almost any other type of business—a fact which the inexperienced city man tends to find hard to accept. A successful farmer, Dr. Walter C. Wood, of New Canaan, Connecticut, a director of Eastern States Farmers' Exchange, was a prominent surgeon in New York City years ago. One of his principal ambitions in life was to be a farmer—an ambition which was finally realized. Some years ago he gave a talk at a gathering of his old medical society. He explained that he had spent about twenty years in the study and practice of surgery, but becoming a surgeon, he stated, was relatively easy compared with what you had to know to be a successful farmer.

A BUSINESS AT HOME

Burt Goodloe, an artist, offers an example of a profession carried on in the country home. His studio is near the small village of Jacksonville, Vermont, on a hillside farm of over one hundred acres. Actually, Burt and Connie Goodloe use only a small portion of their acreage. They have a large garden, a family cow, chickens, a steer, and some dwarf trees. Eventually the Goodloes plan to build another house and find a hired man to help do some commercial farming. There are few sections in the country, however, where land is cheap enough to enable the average man to have enough acreage so that he can have a large farm simply as a home, with the idea of some day operating it as a going farm.

Today the biggest opportunities in the country are in the rural service field, rather than in farming itself. No less an authority than the *New York Times* said: "The tremendous scope of the rural service field is visualized by few. In the years ahead it is certain to include more frozen food company locker plants, rural electrification, custom work with power machinery for farmers who prefer to hire rather than own, scientific soil conservation, modern forestry, and refrigeration, road-side stands. . .

"It seems evident that we are ready for a great expansion toward higher standards of country living. It does not mean more farmers. It does mean many more part-time country homes on roads radiating from cities and larger towns."

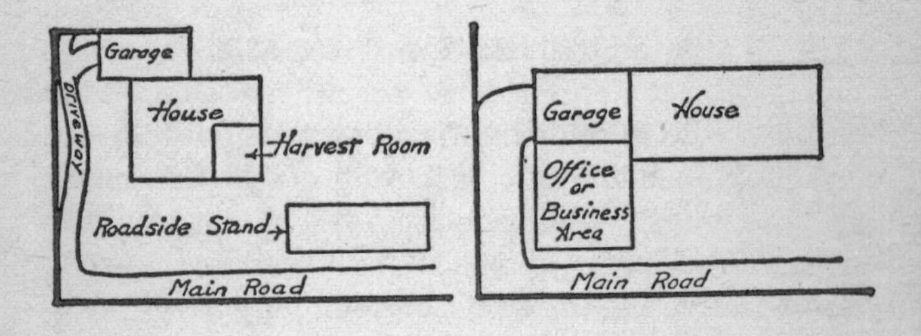

The position of a country home with respect to the road may be influenced by the needs of a part or full-time business. The layout at the left enables watching a roadside stand from the kitchen or "harvest room." At the right, an office or shop is combined with a house.

The next time you ride through the country, notice the many signs along the road put up by people who are operating little businesses of their own. You will see the country lawyer, the country doctor, the country radio repair man, the country beauty and barber shop, the country store, the plumber, the upholsterer, the photographer, and so on—just as if a classified directory list had come to life.

Most of these places have considerable land around them for food production.

THE CHANGING RETIREMENT HOME

Formerly most people didn't retire until late in life. Now, with social security, the increased popularity of retirement income insurance, civil service, military pensions, the many pension plans of industries, millions can look forward to a small regular income at an earlier retirement age. This income begins early enough to enable people to enjoy it through useful activity.

You are familiar, of course, with the advertisements picturing middle-aged couples having a fabulous time fishing, travelling, enjoying the seashore, or just loafing. But a careful look at what people do when they retire shows that they do not stop living productively. Here is a sample of what I mean: A friend of mine attended a Grange meeting in Dutchess County, New York, at which the county agent spoke to a group of poultrymen. He was amazed to see that nearly half the audience was composed of retired businessmen. They were the ones who were showing the keenest interest, asking the questions, and taking notes. He learned that some of these "retired businessmen" were having greater success with their poultry farms than many of the professional poultrymen!

One of the leading farm magazines recently pointed out that retiring farmers are no longer all moving to town. Many are now building small houses with every modern convenience right on their farms. Their sons are taking over, while they continue to help, giving the young folks encouragement and the benefit of their hard-earned experience.

But these are extremes. The average family retiring to the country is more interested in living in the country as a way of life than in farming. And because they have the advantage of a cash income, they are enjoying all the fun offered by this way of life without worrying too much about the business aspects of farming. Those who have been interested in some particular phase of agriculture often devote their time to developing it into a hobby, doing interesting experimental work in the development of new fruits, plants, flowers, bees, poultry and livestock.

The young or middle-aged man who can arange to put his spare time and money into developing and paying for a productive country home can use even a small pension or annuity payment to retire years earlier. With no rent, no large capital outlay, and the ability to raise their food, a couple can live comfortably, free of worries, on a small assured income.

THE SECOND HOME

Within recent years there has been a tremendous upsurge of interest in the second home for leisure living. Its appeal has grown as modern highways, small airports, and three-day weekends have made owning a second home in the country more feasible.

There are many reasons why a person may decide to buy a second home. Some land is bought primarily as an investment; if this is your motivation, then you will need to be extremely careful, as your piece of property may not have the potential to turn a profit.

More often, however, the second home in the country is regarded as a place to escape from the rapid pace of the city and the weekday pressures. In this case, the buyer should give as careful consideration to the explanations given in this book, as if he were buying a permanent home. After all, it is the rare man who wishes to spend his weekends in the country working on never completed repairs.

The individual deciding on a second home should have a clear idea of how he wishes to spend his leisure time. If he wishes to use it as a weekend "escape," he must decide just how far he is willing to travel on a Friday afternoon to get there. If he plans on using it for a summer home, he must evaluate the recreational resources available. Are the size and location of the site conducive to indulging in his hobbies of swimming, bird-watching, gardening?

Often, the buyer of the second home is thinking ahead to retirement, and thus has many aspects to consider. What may be an ideal vacation retreat in the summer could be poorly suited to year-round living. Thus, when buying a second home, one must be aware of present needs in leisure living, and potential future use of the home.

Chapter Two

HOW TO DECIDE WHAT YOU CAN AFFORD

One of the first problems to confront a family when it seriously considers the business of buying country property is: "How much can we afford to spend?"

Most counsel on the subject dismisses this vastly important matter by offering certain "rule-of-thumb" formulas as to the relationship between income and the amount which can be spent. These rule-of-thumb recommendations are useful if used with caution and knowledge of the exceptions to the rule.

It is when you finally start to figure what you can afford to spend that the struggle takes place between large dreams and practical needs, between desires and actual resources, between present and probable future income. And it is at this very point that reality must exert its influence.

As a brake against your own optimism, a check against that of the real estate man, and a stimulus to any misgivings you might have as to whether you *can* afford a country home, we will give you in this chapter the approximate limits of investment which the experience of innumerable property owners has found practicable over many years, through good times and bad. They are not rigid, and we will try to point out the variable factors that you will do well to consider in arriving at your decision. But by and large we should definitely recommend that you stay within the suggested limits of investment.

There are two factors that are basic in computing your ability to pay for country property:

(1) Your present resources.
(2) Your annual cash income.

No doubt both represent actual earnings—the one past, the other present and future. Your present resources, represented by savings and other liquid assets, will be used to make the cash down payment on your property. They will determine what relation the down payment will bear to the mortgage. If your assets exceed by an appreciable margin the cost of your property, cash payment in full is unquestionably the best policy. To those who have more cash than is actually needed for a substantial down payment, and who will have no trouble securing a mortgage, it is well to allow for a fairly substantial fluid cash reserve. No person inexperienced in country living, and, as a matter of fact, few experienced ones, can anticipate all the many expenses that may turn up unpredictably the first few years in a new place.

YOUR PRESENT FINANCIAL CONDITION

It is a good idea, therefore, to begin with an objective look at your present financial picture. You can rest assured that when you *do* apply for a mortgage the lending institution *will* look into this. And you will find that they are impressed by people who are able to regard their own finances in the cold light of impartial analysis. Get the facts about your present financial situation divorced from any wishful thinking. If your ability to pay is not up to your needs or desires, now is the time to find this out and avoid the embarrassment of having it pointed out to you by the matter-of-fact stranger at the financial institution.

Here is the essential information:

Your Assets

(1) *Your equity in any real estate that you may now own.* Figure the cost to you and the present value of it, estimated at its present selling price, deducting the mortgage and any other encumbrances against it. This will give you the amount of cash you could realize, if you sold your real estate.

(2) *Stocks and bonds that you own*—valued at their present market quotation.

(3) *The cash surrender or loan value of life insurance.*

(4) *Other money expected soon*—such as profits from a going business, figured conservatively, and based on former profits over similar periods and not needed for current expenses; income from *certain* bonuses, royalties, ownership of property other than real estate, such as an automobile having a considerable turn in value, a cabin cruiser, interest in a store or business.

(5) *Money owed you from any source*—such as special services you have rendered, if there is reasonable expectation of your being paid; good loans you have made; mortgages which you may hold, if payment is due shortly.

(6) *Your savings.*

Your Liabilities

(1) *Money which you owe for personal reason*—payments on which are impending.

(2) *Notes or other business obligations*—to banks, individuals, or others; installments on automobiles, furniture, unpaid balances for land, equipments, etc.

(3) *Any other liabilities, present or future*—such as judgments or impending lawsuits on which judgment might be based, etc.

It is the difference between your assets and liabilities, of course, that will show your real financial worth, and determine pretty much what you can do in the matter of making a payment on your country property.

There is another element which enters into a consideration of your "worth"—an intangible element—whether it falls into the area of lending money or any other transaction. That is your "moral worth," referred to by lending institutions as "moral risk." Insurance companies and financial institutions always take moral risk into consideration when issuing policies or making a loan. It is a little hard to define moral risk briefly. It involves the risk the insurance company or the lending institution must take with your personal character—your sense of responsibility and the dependability you have shown in meeting obligations. It is because of this intangible element that one man may walk into a bank with what seems to be fairly good assets and get a closely-figured loan, while another, applying at the same bank, with little to show beyond his past business history, is able to get a *substantial* loan.

This factor means that if you are a good "moral risk" you can benefit from this happy circumstance in negotiating a mortgage. But that is getting ahead of our story; our immediate concern is with how much down payment you can make, and this is determined not by your moral assets but by your liquid assets—those that can be turned into cash.

Cash may be secured, as you know, by selling stocks and bonds, including war bonds, real estate or other personal property, by selling your interest in a business or in estates, and through many other transactions with which you are no doubt familiar. Among these are borrowing—but that is a very dubious means of raising funds for making a down payment on property. In addition to the obligations incurred through the purchase, you will be faced by the need of paying interest and repaying the principal of the loan.

CASH VALUE OF INSURANCE

As you know, most life insurance policies have what is known as a cash surrender value. This is generally equivalent to the amount paid by you in cash over a period of years. Your policy probably gives information regarding its cash surrender value, or you may check with the company. Most insurance companies will lend you the amount of this cash surrender value, charging a regular rate of interest. If the policy is not fully paid up, you will be required, naturally to continue to make regular premium payments. If the policy is paid up, no further payments will be required, of course. Under either plan your insurance protection continues. The amount of the loan you make would be deducted, however, from the full value of your insurance, should anything happen to you.

A bank, also, will lend you the amount of the cash surrender value of your life insurance, less the amount of one annual premium. The reason for retaining this annual premium is the fact that if you default in paying the premium, the bank will pay it to keep the policy in force. Of course, if you allowed your premium to lapse, quite probably the bank would demand the full amount of their loan.

If you borrowed against your policy from the bank, you would have to assign your policy to them, so that the bank could be secured to the extent of the loan and premium payment. This would in no way affect the value of your insurance policy. In considering a loan on your life insurance policies compare the interest rate charged by the insurance company as against that of the bank. These rates often vary. You would naturally negotiate the loan offering the lowest rate of interest. Borrowing on life insurance, however, is not greatly advised.

Banks will lend money on stocks, bonds, etc. Probably 75 per cent of their current market value would be the maximum loaned. In a wildly fluctuating market the maximum would be less—perhaps 50 per cent. The bank would, most probably, with such loans, ask that you sign a "demand note" for the value of the loan. This means that you would be required to pay to the bank the full amount of the loan on such stocks or bonds at any time the bank demanded it, as would happen if the market price of the securities fell to any substantial extent.

It is doubtful whether a bank would lend you much on assets such as possible income from royalties, money owed you, money anticipated from estates, etc. They recognize that the prospect of such income makes for a more stable financial position on your part, but they prefer to rely on such assets as could be converted into cash quickly and readily, in the event the borrower defaults the interest-payment or repayment of any money loaned.

CASH RESERVES

The figure reached by deducting your liabilities from your assets is called your "net worth." While we have advocated making as large a down payment on your country property as is reasonably possible, we believe that it is unwise in most cases to consider the total of your net worth as the sum available for down payment on your property. It is vitally important, if you are to be free of worry, to retain part of your cash or assets in the form of a contingency fund or savings to cover any emergency, such as illness, accident or unemployment or any situation that might require an appreciable amount of cash.

And don't forget that in the actual transaction of buying country property there are a number of expenses which occur *in addition* to the actual down payment on the property—legal matters, investigation, recording expenses, etc. These will be discussed in full on succeeding pages.

In addition to a cash reserve for emergencies, money will be needed if you contemplate undertaking the establishment of a business in the country. Milton Wend, author of "How to Live in the Country without Farming," has given much study to the subject; he advises that a family considering buying country property without an assured cash income should retain in the bank a sum adequate to provide modest living expenses for a period of at least a year and a half. "Practically no venture," says Mr. Wend, "pays a profit the first year, whether of family-size or a million dollar enterprise."

RATIO OF DOWN PAYMENT

Remembering our counsel that it is best to pay all cash, if possible, and in any event to retain a savings or contingency fund over and above the payment, the question arises as to how *much* the down payment on country property should be in the interests of safety and wisdom.

There are certain irreducible minimums below which it isn't regarded as prudent to go. Despite the fact that FHA insured loans and GI loans enable you to make a down payment of from nothing at all to 10 per cent or more, most banks ask that the minimum down payment on property should be at least 25 per cent of the total cost of the property, including the cost of the land. For example, on land costing $1,500 with a house existing or to be constructed on that land, valued at or to cost $35,000, making a total investment of $36,500, most banks ask for a down payment of not less than $9,125. This they regard as the absolute minimum to insure safety and peace of mind for you as well as for them. The more the payment, the better.

We don't mean to imply at all that perfectly sound purchases haven't been made through the FHA and GI loans with a down payment of 10 per cent, especially if the borrowers were young, vigorous, able, responsible, hard-working people. Such loans have been and will continue to be paid off. Young people have been able to assume responsibilities so large as to appall a more seasoned family with a conservative outlook. For the older and well-established family a down payment of less than 25 per cent could well be a source of worry and heartache that would offset all the satisfactions of country-home ownership. Never forget that the larger the down payment, the lighter the burden of debt and "carrying charges."

CARRYING CHARGES vs. ANNUAL CASH INCOME

We have considered, now, the method of establishing your financial worth, and of approximating the amount of down payment you are able to make on country property. If you can safely devote $9,000, say to the initial payment, this—at the rate of 25 per cent of the whole price—*may* enable you to buy a place with a total cost of $36,000 with all the "extras" included. We say "may" because in the final analysis your ability to buy a place with a mortgage depends upon your ability to meet the carrying charges, and this in turn depends upon your income and how much of it you can devote to all the things involved in sheltering your family. It is all too easy to buy property at an unwarranted cost simply because of your ability to make a relatively high down payment.

YOUR ANNUAL CASH INCOME

At this point, it is well to take a look at your anticipated cash income as it relates to your ability to incur obligations. If you are moving to the country from one of the smaller cities and plan to commute to your present job or you are buying a second home, you can expect that your income will remain steady or increase through the years. For many of you, however, moving will mean finding a new job or setting up your own business. Your annual income may be less than you are now earning, with unpredictable fluctuations as you become established. It would be advisable to find employment before buying your property, renting a house or apartment in the neighborhood where you hope to live. In this way you can discover if this is really the place where you want to live, while learning what you can expect to earn. If you are going into business on your own, substantial savings (enough to support you for one to two years), or outside income will be necessary. When considering what you can afford use very conservative figures in estimating future income.

In attempting to predict the effect of the years ahead on income, differences will be evident as between the younger and the older man. Granted that both are starting their country homes at the same time, the younger man can look forward to a longer earning span than the older man. It would seem, at first glance, as though he should be able to assume a larger obligation. But in the long run his larger earnings may become absorbed by a long and steady drain on his earnings to cover expenses which the older man has already met. The younger man may have furniture to buy, children to bring up, the education of his children to be arranged for; he will want some travel and more recreation.

The need for conservatism hardly needs to be stressed for the older man. Except in unusual cases, there will be little increase in earning or saving power, say after fifty. There is always more chance of protracted illness, hospitalization, unemployment—besides fluctuations if you are in business for yourself. For these and other reasons it is hoped that the older man will not only stay within the most conservative limits of homestead investment, but that he will limit as far as possible the time of repayment of mortgages if a loan is necessary!

ABOUT A BUDGET

Whatever the figure you arrive at for annual cash income, the next step is to deduct income taxes from it and you cannot safely consider that taxes will be very materially reduced for a number of years to come.

Then draw up a budget, if you don't already have one, which will show your current family "running expenses." Include all these items: food, clothing, gas and electricity, telephone, furniture, replacements; medical and educational expenses; insurance, taxes other than income taxes, charity, a vacation, other recreational costs and lunches and other special expenses of the breadwinner, such as carfare. Consider what *increased* expenses might lie ahead, such as for the care of children or an elderly relative.

Whatever is left after these deductions from your cash income is the amount available for savings and shelter, and thus, in a sense, the amount you can figure on for the carrying charges of buying a country place (except in the case of the second home).

But the budget needs translation to the special conditions of country living, and this is a little hard to figure in advance. You will need a car whether or not you commute; if you use the car to go to and from work it will cost you about 10 cents a mile. If you plan to start a business, you will need to provide for that.

Then there are certain installations you are going to want on your country property—if it is going to be productive property. You will need lumber, perhaps, for a small barn or chicken house you want to build.

There will be equipment, a freezer, livestock, fruit trees, seeds and fertilizer to buy—perhaps a garden tractor, or a trailer.

"But," you may say, "these are mostly productive items which should more than pay for themselves. Can't I count on big savings on food costs?"

This is the answer: in the long run, you should be able to realize material savings, and they will give you real security and satisfaction. But it isn't safe to count on them at the outset. For some period of time the savings will be held down by the natural inefficiency of the beginner and perhaps more than offset by the expenses of getting started. It is better to let them come as a bonus, a reward for your decisions to work at the Garden Way of living—the equivalent, in short, of a big raise in salary! For maximum security, plan to use the prospective savings in mortgage reduction.

ABOUT CARRYING CHARGES

The use here of the term "carrying charges" is a bit different from the way it is often used by real estate agents. They like to keep the figure as low as possible, for obvious reasons, and they go to the extent sometimes of considering only interest and mortgage amortization payments as "carrying charges." These, they may tell you, are the equivalent of the rent you pay in a city apartment—an entirely unsound comparison.

True carrying charges cover all your shelter items, hence real estate taxes, interest, repayment of mortgage, insurance on buildings, repairs and maintenance, plus heating, water and light. Almost all these, you will observe, are items which the city landlord absorbs out of the rent you pay him.

TAXES

Town or township tax rates are subject to revision from time to time, but not enough to make a significant difference in the amount you must set aside weekly or monthly for real estate taxes. Rates vary from 1 to 5 per cent of the appraised value of the property. This is the value set by the local tax assessor or collector. In other words, if your property is appraised by the town as having a value of $20,000 and the tax rate is 3 per cent you would pay 3 per cent of $20,000 a year, or $600, a "carrying charge" of $50 a month.

In some areas, such as Vermont, the tax assessors—called "Listers"—are required by state law to appraise property at its full fair market value. If you pay considerably more for a piece of property than its appraisal, you can expect that your tax appraisal and taxes will be higher than they were for the previous owner.

In other areas the assessed valuation of property is quite a bit lower than the market value of it. Taxes may be just as high, however, depending on the local tax rate.

INSURANCE

Every house should have fire insurance, the rate depending on the material of which the house is built, the fire-fighting facilities of the township, and other considerations. A good country rate might be one-half of one per cent of the property value. Some lending institutions include fire insurance premiums in the amount they collect monthly. Fire insurance must be figured as a fixed charge, although this is generally a small sum.

HEATING

Heating costs must be taken into consideration in most parts of the country. It isn't easy to determine accurately what it will cost each year to heat a house. Heating costs might be estimated at from 1½ per cent of the value of the house in cold climates, to ½ per cent in warm climates, with wide variations, depending upon the type of heating system, and the cost of heating a $20,000 house in cold climates would be approximately $300 a year.

There is a better method of checking this, however. Inquiry in the locality will usually give you the average heating cost for a four-, five-, or six-room house with various types of fuels—about the same for each fuel. If your house is very much like the neighboring ones, your costs will be approximately the same. In the average locality heating costs rarely fall below an average of $20 a month.

REPAIRS, ETC.

You will do well to estimate from $20 to $30 a month for repairs, painting and other maintenance items. Actual costs will depend on the condition of the property and how much work you do yourself.

GAS AND ELECTRICITY

These costs vary widely. It is best to figure them as 50 per cent more than you pay in the city. Rural rates are often lower but you will probably find you are using more current under country living conditions than in the city.

RULES OF THUMB

We have shown as clearly as possible how to figure the down payment you can make and how much in the form of monthly shelter charges you can carry—also how to estimate some of these charges. But perhaps you would prefer to go at the question of how much you can pay in a different way.

Maybe you would rather wait, before getting into the intricacies of budgeting and figuring carrying charges, until you have seen the country home you would like to own—because then you will be able to figure prospective costs more closely. You want a rough figure to shoot at, for your own guidance and that of the real estate agents.

For this purpose we have the rules of thumb we mentioned at the outset of this chapter. We believe that all the considerations we have brought up already make it clear that any generalizations are likely to be misleading and must be double-checked against individual circumstances. In addition, the rules are the outgrowth of experience with suburban properties, and therefore may not be so good a guide to the buying of country property. With these reservations, here we go:

The experience of many home buyers over the years has shown that the total cost of a house *and* land, complete with fixtures, lighting, plumbing—ready to move into—*should not exceed two or two-and-a-half-times your annual cash income after taxes.* Real estate brokers may tell you that you can expend up to three times your annual cash income. Conservative bankers, on the other hand, insist that one-and-two-thirds times your annual cash income is the safest figure. Only a careful analysis, study and *application of the factors existing in your own financial setup* will enable you to arrive at the right amount for you.

In the table below we give you as a guide the amount you may spend for your country property, based on your annual cash income, using conservative, average, liberal and high ratios:

Table 1

If *annual income after taxes is:*	At the rate of *1⅔* annual income you may buy property at not more than:	At the rate of *twice* annual income you may buy property at not more than:	At the rate *2½ times* annual income you may buy property at not more than:	At the rate *3 times* annual income you may buy property at not more than:
	(Conservative)	(Average)	(Liberal)	(High)
$ 5,000	$ 8,333	$10,000	$12,500	$15,000
7,000	11,686	14,000	17,500	21,000
10,000	16,666	20,000	25,000	30,000
15,000	24,999	30,000	41,500	45,000

Here are some of the obvious modifications of these figures for country as against typical suburban living:

(1) Not immediately, but eventually, substantial, savings in food costs will enable the Garden Wayer, if he so chooses, to devote a larger proportion of his income to shelter than can the owner of a non-productive home.

(2) Use of the country home for a part-time business, will add to the owner's income, if the business is successful.

(3) Use of the country home for a full-time business, or for retirement, will reduce or eliminate travel costs, especially commuting, cancelling one of the normal debits of the suburban budget.

(4) Savings on recreation and entertainment may be substantial in the country, where many activities and sports can be enjoyed free in your own back-yard or neighborhood.

(5) Country taxes are sometimes a good deal lower than suburban taxes.

There are possible exceptions to the rule that it is best not to go over the "2 or 2½ times income" ceiling. You may be the spartan type, for instance, who is willing to forego luxuries and hold expenditures on necessities way below average levels, thus changing the usual budget relationships and enabling the purchase of a more costly piece of property than an income the size of yours would ordinarily warrant.

If your after tax income is less than $5,000 a year, you may find it impossible to secure suitable country property within the conservative ratio figures of Table 1. You will have three choices:

(1) Somehow increase your income.
(2) Wait until you have saved enough to make such a large down payment that the carrying charges on the property you want are not too burdensome.
(3) Make the necessary sacrifice in living expenses, and take the necessary risk in buying over the conservative figure.

MORE "RULE-OF-THUMB" RATIOS

Suppose you were to figure that you can pay one-and-two-thirds or twice your annual income for your house and land. That isn't all the figuring you need to do to obtain a true picture of what you can reasonably afford to pay for country property.

It has been held that for people who rent apartments or houses the *monthly rent* should not exceed one week's salary. It has been similarly estimated that the total *monthly* carrying charges for country property should not exceed your income for *one week or ten days* —that is, your *cash* income, after taxes.

Based on the foregoing:

Table 2

If income after taxes is:	At the rate of 1 week's income your limit on "carrying" charges will be:	At the rate of 10 days' income your limit will be:
$ 5,000	$ 96.15 a month	$137.30/mo.
7,000	134.46 a month	192.10/mo.
10,000	192.30 a month	274.70/mo.
15,000	288.45 a month	411.90/mo.

Another rule of thumb is the well-established one that you can comfortably afford to pay for house and land 100 times what you pay for *rental* housing in a month.

On the basis of your annual income (after taxes), Table 1 helps you determine what you should pay for country property on a conservative, average, liberal, and maximum basis, merely by simple multiplication.

Table 2 helps you to determine whether the "carrying charges" on property that you are considering will be too large or too small for you to carry, based on your annual cash income.

Table 3 will help you determine what the equivalent would be in home ownership to your present living costs (if you live in a rented house or apartment).

Table 3

Under this rule of 100:

If your monthly rent were:	You could afford to pay 100 times that amount for house and land.
$ 80.00	$ 8,000
100	10,000
135	13,500
175	17,500
225	22,500
275	27,500
350	35,000

You may find that these tables don't agree on the exact amount you can afford to pay. But you will probably find that the three different ways of estimating your limits will come remarkably close to agreeing!

Now, a final reminder that if you are not able to pay cash, the most important question in property financing lies in determining whether the job or profession you now have in the city, or expect to get in the country, will pay enough over a period of years to meet the principal, interest, and "carrying charges" on your property. If you have a steady job or income, you can secure your homestead by regular payments, even if the ratio between your down payment and mortgage is slightly out of balance. On the other hand, with an unsteady income, even if your equity in the homestead is very high, you may be unable to meet your mortgage payments and may lose the homestead.

The material in this chapter should emphasize for you the imperative need for spending a good deal of time and hard thought in getting the facts of your financial situation down in black and white, so that you will know, within limits, just how much you can afford to pay when buying your country property.

Chapter Three

HOW TO GET THE MOST OUT OF REAL ESTATE MEN

Your best aid in finding country property will be a real estate man, so perhaps you had better get to know him —or his kind—pretty early in your search. You have the right, of course, to consult as many agents as you please. You *should* consult them in several localities, and even several in the same locality. It is both right and wise to see as large a variety of properties in any locality of your choice as you can, so as to get a real knowledge of land and property values in the area. Give one or two agents a reasonable time to look for something for you. If they don't succeed, feel entirely free to turn to others.

Don't let one agent take you to see property that another has previously shown you, however. Should you decide to buy that particular piece of property, there is likely to be an argument as to which agent is entitled to the commission.

Don't begrudge a real estate broker his commission. Let him *earn* it, though. See that he puts his knowledge to work for *you,* even though his natural tendency is to serve the *seller* primarily, since he gets his commission from the seller. The amount of his commission will be about 6% of the sale price of land with building, or as much as 10% on land that has no improvements on it.

The real estate broker has acquired knowledge about property in his vicinity which you would undoubtedly never gain. He has seen hundreds of pieces of property to your one. He has *bought* and *sold* hundreds. He knows the history of practically every piece of property in the locality; who owned it previously; who owns it now; the trouble people have had with it, and, what is most important, its real market value at the present time. Knowing the owner, and probably a good deal about him, the real estate broker has a pretty good idea of how much below his asking price the owner will actually take.

The real estate broker knows more. He knows the way the locality is expanding; the history of its taxes and assessments; what improvements and assessments are being planned; even what the operating costs and profits of farms have been. And, if necessary, the real estate broker can help you a great deal with your financing. City banks have never been eager to lend money on country property. Often the broker can introduce you to a local lending institution, which, if the conditions are satisfactory, will agree to a mortgage.

In a housing shortage—such as we now have—the

real estate broker isn't going to turn any handsprings when you come to him with $1,000 to $5,000 worth of business. This undoubtedly is a temporary situation, and the intelligent real estate agent tries to keep enough balance in his listings so that he can show some properties to any kind of prospect. But there is no gain–saying the fact that it takes him just about as long to sell a $25,000 piece of property as it does a $40,000 piece. What he will do for you depends on his volume of business and the type of property he customarily handles.

GETTING ACQUAINTED WITH THE AGENT

Call the agent for an appointment, if possible. Remember that his busy days are Saturday and Sunday, so if you can, make the appointment for a week-day. Also, if you can manipulate it, see a country real estate man in the fall or winter. Country property is generally cheaper and easier to buy in the fall or winter. The spring is the agent's rush season.

Get across to the agent the fact that you are serious about buying country property. Particularly over pleasant weekends, country brokers are sought out so often by passing motorists idly inquiring about country property that it is not uncommon for them to find that while they may have talked to a hundred or more people, less than a handful of them were seriously considering buying.

If instead of walking into his office "cold," you have been recommended to him by the local bank, the Chamber of Commerce, the National Association of

Real Estate Boards, perhaps a mutual friend, let him know that. Tell him frankly that you have had difficulty finding the kind of country property you have had your mind set on, and that he has been recommended by so-and-so as *one* real estate operator who will really make an effort to get you what you want. Flattery never did hurt a real estate man. He gets so little of it he will appreciate it no end!

BE SPECIFIC

Next, be frank and specific. Don't try to give the agent the impression that you are a millionaire traveling incognito, nor, on the contrary, that you are on the verge of bankruptcy. Sooner or later he will find out just how much you can spend, so don't try to keep it a dark secret. Give him your maximum price, and let it *be* your maximum. If you have assured him that you don't want to spend more than $15,000, and then proceed to show an interest in a $19,000 piece of property, he will justifiably begin to lose confidence in your word and ignore your stipulated maximum.

Be as specific as possible in presenting your requirements. Explain as clearly as you can the purpose for which you want the property. For example, productive homesteading may be a new term to many agents, and some of them won't quite "get it." But if you make it clear that you just want to raise your own food; that you aren't going to sell much produce (unless you eventually want either a part-time or full-time farm), and that you are not in the market for a country estate, he *may* get the idea.

All agents aren't equally efficient or reliable. You can, of course, by some stroke of luck, buy a good piece of property through a poor agent, but you are more likely to buy it through a good one. In some localities, usually in resort or suburban sections, there are "curbstone" agents with offices in their hats. You will get to know them by their lack of organization, by the appearance of their offices, and by their general ineptitude. In many suburbs and country districts, where there is no licensing of real estate brokers, anyone can announce himself or herself a real estate agent merely by hanging out a shingle. You won't be likely to get good property by doing business with a housewife who may sell several pieces of property a year for pin money!

The average realty agent is neither badly intentioned nor dishonest. He is, however, likely to "ride" your enthusiasm about a place, for, after all, his very livelihood depends upon his selling property. However, an honest and painstaking broker, of which there are many, will not only readily admit disadvantages in a piece of property, but will often advise against certain properties as unrelated to your expressed desires and needs.

Don't be afraid of criticizing property for fear of hurting the real estate broker's feelings. He is quite accustomed to honest criticism, and it is only by your frank and open criticism that he can get a comprehensive idea of just what you are looking for.

OPTIMISTS AND PESSIMISTS

As in all other professions, there are optimists and pessimists in the real estate business. The pessimist is always "just out of what you want," or he sold exactly that kind of house and acreage last week. He is always prepared with the ever ready, "I don't think you'll ever find what you want at that price." Or, he may even give up before he starts. He is merely waiting for that "killing" he hopes to make such as selling a big piece of property for a new factory.

The optimistic realtor invariably has "just what you want," and proceeds to show you exactly the opposite. He is the fellow who will try to out-talk, out-ride, and out-wear you. If you keep on looking, slowly and persistently, as counselled in these pages, he is going to let you know, ever so delicately at first, that you are—well, sort of hard to please! The next time it is apt to take the form of his becoming—well, a little discouraged about you. He is going to convey, subtly at first, then a little more openly and sharply, the fact that he has given you a lot of his time; that although he has shown you about everything there is available in the locality, *you* still can't make up your mind. But don't let it worry you. It is the old psychology he is trying to use on you—the old stunt of making you feel under obligation to him. Take your time. Don't be hurried into a decision. It is *your* money you are spending, not his, and remember, *you* had to work just as hard to get it as *he* may have to work to get you what you want!

YOUR WIFE CAN HELP

The agent is going to try psychology on your wife, too. He is going to turn on the old charm to the limit of his capacity. He is going to help her in and out of the car, and hold the door for her as she enters and exits. He is going to comment on how youthful she looks, and with two great big sons, too! He is going to watch her like a hawk when she is enthusiastic about the view, while you are poking about in the cellar or in the swamp. Then he is going to let *her* get to work on you!

The smart thing to do is to let your wife go to work on him. One way to go about this is suggested by H. A. Highstone, in his excellent book on subsistence farming, titled: "Practical Farming for Beginners." Says Mr. Highstone:

"Much more land is always for sale than there are buyers for it. Moreover, always demand much more than you expect to get—it is the only way of getting what you want. Concerning this last piece of advice, and considering that in most cases the business of buying the land will be a matter of an amateur buyer going up against an experienced seller of real estate, it will be well to set up in advance a plan of strategy designed to whittle the odds down to somewhere near even.

"It is easy enough to advise and easy enough to decide upon a hard-boiled course of action, but sometimes difficult to follow through. This is because it is part of the strategy of every real estate agent worthy of the name to maneuver the customer into a position where he feels obligated. Human nature being what it is, all but the experienced buyer are automatically put in a position disadvantageous to their interests the moment such a bit of strategy has been consummated. The prospective amateur buyer who is maneuvered—as he is almost without exception—into a position where he feels he has taken up a great deal of the agent's time and put him to considerable expense in showing property, is almost invariably reluctant to assume the overly critical attitude which may save him a lot of money. Likely as not, he will refrain entirely from the important business of expediently finding fault with a property in which he is interested as a prelude to making an offer below the asking price, or in arguing about interest rates and other important matters. Just why this should be is wholly inexplicable when one analyzes the situation, but it is a common quirk of human nature which others should not be permitted to make capital on.

"For all these reasons, the amateur buyer should conveniently provide himself with a scapegoat, or a sort of devil's advocate, whose function it will be to criticize adversely at every opportunity, and who will be unfavorably impressed by every lot of land examined. Needless to say, the criticisms should not be too strenuous, and should follow the precept that moderation in all things is the wisest principle. This second party had best be some feminine member of the buyer's family—a wife is best, because real estate agents are not at all unaccustomed to having wives of prospective purchasers spoil what might otherwise have been profitable transactions. The agent is always at a disadvantage in arguing with a prospective client's wife, and a smart agent never tries it. The average woman is a much smarter horse-trader than the average man, largely because she is hampered by no subconscious fear of being thought a cheapskate, which is a species of false pride, ingrained in every male. Real estate agents know this better than anyone else, perhaps, which makes this particular bit of strategy almost infallible.

"Consequently even the most inexperienced buyer who might otherwise hesitate a long time before making an offer even slightly below an asking price, can boldly present the most outrageous bid and the most impossible terms, simply by blaming it all on his wife. It is easy for him to keep on the best terms with the real estate agent without weakening his position, if he can explain that his wife simply will not agree to the deal under the price and the terms asked.

"All this may seem labored plotting indeed, but it may easily be rewarded by a saving of $500. It is no mere psychological flight of fancy; it is based on both personal experience and observation."

HOW TO READ AN AD

The larger metropolitan newspapers carry advertisements continually about available country property, but you will have to learn to understand the peculiar jargon used. As a general rule it is the larger and more energetic real estate firms that advertise in such papers. They know very well that many of their advertisements will be read by the city man and his wife, and you can't blame them for describing their properties in terms that they know will appeal to the city man's dreams of a place in the country.

You will be sure to read about the magnificent hilltop view, the babbling brook, the graceful old Colonial house, and the fine old trees, for the real estate man is keenly aware of the fact that these are the things associated with the city family's dream-house in the country. The property that is advertised doesn't give the cold, concrete facts you must have in order to buy intelligently.

Reading between the lines will teach you, after a while, the meaning of terms used by the real estate broker in his ads. A "brook" is anything from a trickling spring to a swamp. "Fine community nearby" may mean anything from a collection of cabins to a smoky manufacturing city. "Improvements" may mean anything added since the Revolution. Of course not all advertisements are as pretentious. Many real estate agencies are quite meticulous in the matter of describing their properties realistically.

If you are looking for a part-time or full-time farm, you are more likely to get accuracy in the catalog descriptions of such properties. There are several large, national, farm real estate agencies with offices in practically every large city, and with representatives in hundreds of towns. These agencies issue large, well-illustrated folders and booklets which describe properties in precise, specific language. As a rule, representatives of these farm agencies are chosen for their knowledge of property in the locality, and for their experience in selling such properties. While the usual common sense to be exercised in all transactions should not be overlooked here, the statements of these farm agents are regarded as pretty responsible.

THE LOCAL PAPER

If you have decided finally on a definite locality in which to look for your country property, you can help yourself appreciably by subscribing to the local daily or weekly paper, even while living in the city. You will learn of active local real estate agents from its advertising columns. You will also read of property offered by individual owners. You will learn, too, of properties *not* advertised in the metropolitan newspapers. And generally descriptions of such properties will be more realistic.

You will accomplish even more than that if you read the local papers. You will get to know the community, its surroundings, and the kind of people who live there. If the local police news reports indicate pretty regularly that certain residents in the Berryville section are frequent visitors before the local judge, you may get the idea that Berryville isn't quite the place for your homestead. If you read in the middle of winter that the folks out on the Brookfield road had a pretty rough time getting through, that's the sort of thing you would be up against if you lived out there. And in the local news you will read about the kind of folks you like, and the localities in which they live. You will even catch something of the "tone" of the town—its activities, its politics, its schools, its social life. You will learn a lot more than just real estate.

You can, if you wish, quietly advertise under a box number for property in the township after you know something about the locality, and after you have had some experience in looking at property.

ASK YOUR FRIENDS

Another method of learning about country property is to ask your friends who already have places in the country. Often they are in a position to hear of property to be offered for sale before the real estate man gets to know about it. They have been through the ordeal of searching, and, presumably, have gained experience which you may lack. At any rate they may have lived long enough in their individual communities to know something of the values there.

Of course the enthusiasms of your friends may not be your own enthusiasms, so that you will have to check their fervor against your own plans and desires. Speak to all of your friends who have places in the country. But here is a note of warning! Think twice about buying the place next door. That may be the surest way of losing a friend!

Sometimes you may be advised by well-intentioned people to deal directly with banks in the hope of getting a good buy on distressed or foreclosure property. But give it a little thought. On those rare occasions when a good piece of property falls into the classification of distress property, it is doubtful that you would have an opportunity to consider it. "Insiders" or local buyers would have signed on the dotted line long before you ever learned about it. Besides, banks usually are more interested in "getting out from under" than in satisfying a buyer. But even with distress or foreclosure property, many banks prefer to work through a local real estate broker. When we are riding the crest of a prosperity wave there is little distress property to speak of, whereas in depression periods property values drop everywhere, so that most property falls more or less into the "distress" class then.

The same is likely to be true of the offices of tax collectors and county treasurers as sources through which to buy country property, and for practically the same reasons. Where a piece of property has been sold because of accumulated taxes, you will find it difficult to get a clear title on the property without becoming involved immediately in a law suit.

WHERE ARE THE SIGNS?

There is lots of land for sale, but there never are many "For Sale" signs in country districts, especially in farm lands. Land represents a farmer's capital. Even if a farmer is in a very tight spot for money, he hesitates to let his neighbors and the community know that he has to sell land to get it. His situation would have to be desperate indeed before he could become reconciled to the need of advertising the sale of part of his land by a "For Sale" sign. But as you drive through the country and come across a nice piece of land that appeals to you—or even a house and land—there is nothing to stop you either from asking whether the house is for sale or finding out who owns the land and getting in touch with the owner. If you are lucky enough to find a desirable piece of property in this way, a place you would really like to own, be sure to take particular pains to ascertain the market value of the property before becoming committed to purchase it.

FOUR WAYS OF CHECKING VALUES

Here are four ways of checking the value of any piece of property:

1. You can get the assessed value of the property

from the town tax office. They will give you the usual percentage of the actual value of the property which the assessment represents. Property in small towns is generally underassessed.

2. You can get an appraisal from the local bank or possibly the lending institution.
3. You can compare the price of the land with the price of similar acreage in the vicinity, and if there is a house on the land, the cost of reproducing the house, as explained in this book.
4. You can hire a local property appraiser or assessor, or perhaps a real estate man on an appraisal fee basis.

SOME USEFUL HINTS

If you are really interested in a particular piece of country property, try to visit it in the fall or winter, when you can see it at its worst. If it appeals to you *then,* it has a pretty good chance of retaining its appeal. Or look at it on a gray, rainy day. Almost any kind of property looks attractive in the spring or summer, particularly if you have driven out from the hot, humid city. *Don't* buy by mood or season.

Try to avoid buying "key land." This is the first land down any road, adjoining the property which faces the main road. Your outlook on one side will be toward the main road and the rear of the corner property—usually not the most pleasant outlook. If you do consider a side road, locate further down the road.

Try to disassociate the buying of your homestead

from the idea that the land or location may increase in value, either because of the growth of the town, or because of expanding commercial use. A change from a residential to a commercial zone is a very slow one, generally, and in the span between full residence and full commercial use a long period of time usually elapses, when the neighborhood can't quite make up its mind as to what it is going to be. During this long period prices are likely to continue moderate. It is not until a section is fully built up, in any event, that the prices rise for commercial use.

Residential property values rise slowly, too, and this rise is often offset by increased taxes and assessments paid while it is rising. But aside from such consideration, don't lose sight of the fact that if you buy your country property primarily for productive homestead use, the encroachment of commercial and town or city expansion may well destroy the use and pleasure of your location for your own purposes. It would be more desirable, it would seem, to choose a location that is likely to retain its homesteading character.

And don't buy country property to "surprise" your wife. *You* will probably be the surprised one when you wake up with a cooler head and realize what you have bought.

We have urged much caution in buying your country property. We don't feel that we have stressed it unduly. When, after looking at a piece of country property, you reach the point where you feel that you can come pretty close to estimating its real value; when your family's ideas have crystallized so that you know exactly what you want, then only are you ready to buy. Then when the opportunity of a real bargain comes along, *don't hesitate!* Buy! Bargains near cities are rare. They do occur occasionally, and you should take full advantage if you come across one.

In conclusion, remember that the average buyer does better to buy country property through a real estate broker. To be sure, the real estate broker gets his commission from the seller. He is, in the final analysis, working for the seller rather than the buyer. But it does take two to make the bargain. The real estate agent is fully aware of your stake in the transaction, and of the fact that the deal cannot be consummated until you are satisfied as well.

As far as the agent's commission is concerned, any fairly competent agent can save you the equivalent of his commission through his knowledge of comparative values and his local connections. Once he realizes that you know what you want, that you are aware of what influences property values, and that you are honest with him as well as the seller, he can be of inestimable help to you. It is virtually an invariable rule that property which is offered direct, to "save the broker's fee," is overpriced. There may be other factors concerning the property about which you know nothing, but of which the local broker would be instantly aware.

Don't let anyone tempt you to enter into any "side deals" either with the real estate broker or the seller on any piece of property. You can be perfectly honest with both the seller and the real estate man without losing any of your shrewdness or bargaining ability. Try to hold as little in reserve from them regarding your wants and financial ability as possible, and you will be perfectly within your rights to expect an equal amount of frankness and honesty on their part.

Chapter Four

FACTS TO REMEMBER ABOUT LAND

When you buy property in the average city, suburb, or development, little or no consideration is given to the land on which a house stands, or on which a house is to be built. In buying country property, however, especially with a *productive* homestead in mind, land becomes most important, not only with reference to its location, but from the point of view of the vegetable and animal life it may have to support. Houses can be built, rebuilt, remodelled and repaired, but, as somebody has said, "It takes a thousand years to make an inch of topsoil."

Families accustomed to living in cities are likely to think of land in terms of lots. Residential lots in cities and suburbs are commonly 50 feet wide by 100 feet deep. This "front-foot" method of computation is resorted to so as to enable the developer to get as many lots fronting on the street as possible. In the more expensive outlying areas, zoning may require that each residence occupy two lots. In the still more restricted suburbs, regulations may demand that residences occupy a minimum of a half acre or more of land.

Country property—productive country property in particular—is figured in terms of acres. If you have never given much thought to the size of an acre, it might be well for you to become accustomed to visualizing it. If you remember your arithmetic, an acre contains 43,560 square feet. An acre of land, if perfectly square, would occupy a space about 208 x 208 feet. You can "pace off" an acre by taking 70 paces at an average length of 3 feet, and then continuing to pace 70 paces at right angles until you return to your starting point. It may make it easier to visualize an acre when we tell you that it is about the size of the average football field. You can readily see, then, that an acre is a pretty sizable piece of land. Perhaps that will enable you to understand how so many homesteaders are able to do so much with two or three acres.

After you have had the experience of pacing off a few acres, and when you have looked at more land, seeing it in terms of acreage rather than mere stretches of land, you will be able to estimate fairly accurately how large a given tract is. To help you to determine the number of acres there are in a given piece of country property of irregular dimension, you will find a handy acreage chart on page 60 with full directions as to its use.

THE PRICE OF ACREAGE

The price of land generally varies in accordance with the density of population. On Wall Street in New York City, and in the Loop in Chicago, the price is figured by the front *foot*—almost by the inch—and is fabulous! As you reach residential areas and suburbs the price is figured by the lot. The average city lot of 50 x 100 feet contains 5,000 square feet, which means that it would take about 8½ city lots to make an acre. In the average suburban development small lots run in price from $1500 to $3000. Figured on the basis of the cost of the average suburban lot, the price per acre would run from $12,750 to $25,500, obviously very high for homestead purposes.

Because of the need of having an acre or more of land for real country living, it will be necessary for you to get far enough away from the city so that land ceases being apportioned in lots and is sold, rather, by the acre. But even here the distance from the city will determine the cost per acre. At the point where expensive suburbs "end," the cost may be $10,000 for one acre. It will drop gradually in price, then, as the distance from commuting facilities and city centers increases.

For the family planning a retirement home, the price of land will not be a problem. Since they may go beyond the commuting zones of cities for their land, they may be able to buy a good acre of land, for $800 to $2,000. A part-time or commercial farmer will have to give considerable thought to the price of his land, as it represents his capital investment. The price of

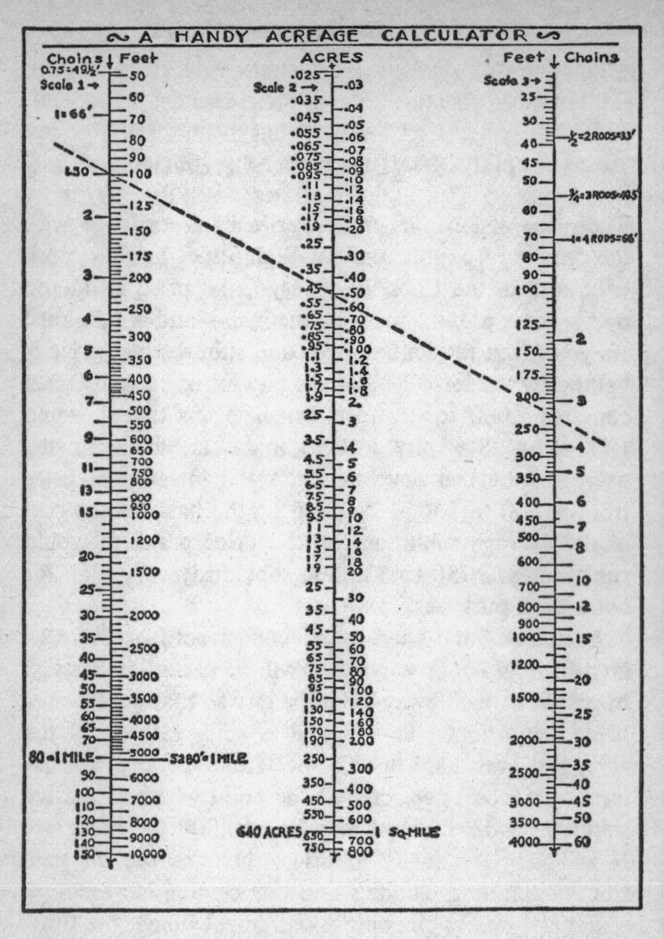

To find the acreage of a rectangular piece of land, mark one dimension on the column at the left, the other on the column at the right, and draw a straight line between them. Where the line crosses the central column is the approximate area in acres. If land is odd shape, divide into smaller areas, each as nearly rectangular as possible and add up to get total area. (The dotted line shows that a piece 100x230 ft. measures about one-half acre.

productive farm land in the country runs from $50 to $100 in large pieces, on the western ranches to around $2,000 in Lancaster County, Pennsylvania. Land prices rise as the farm land nears the city. Sometimes this higher cost is offset by the good roads and the proximity of the farm to markets. The relationship of the price of farm land to the total farm investment is amply covered in specialized books on farm management for prospective farmers. For the average homesteader the maximum price paid for a single acre of land should not exceed $5,000—preferably it should be less. When more than one acre is purchased the average price per acre would decrease proportionately.

HOW MUCH LAND?

It is wise to buy more land than you expect to use productively. The extreme of too little land should be avoided. At the risk, perhaps, of being too specific:

—A "spare-time" homestead might have from a half acre to an acre, perhaps up to three acres.

—A fully productive homestead, or a retirement homestead, or a part-time farm, allowing for the raising of most of your food, plus food for your livestock, might have from three to twelve acres.

—A small, full-time farm might have twelve acres or more.

If you contemplate having a beef steer or milk cow as part of your homestead, and are considering growing your own feed, it will be necessary for you to have one or two acres of pasture land and about two acres for a hayfield. To make two goats or two sheep self-sustaining on your homestead, you would require half to one acre of pasture land and about an acre for your hayfield.

If land costs per acre were within reason, and taxes in the locality weren't too high, you might consider buying extra acreage for expansion or other usage, especially if you have reason to believe the location may develop into a vacation area. You can invariably do very much better as far as price per acre is concerned if you buy a larger piece of land. When you buy less acreage with the expectation of expanding at some future time, you may have to pay an appreciably higher price for the adjoining land. The owner of the adjoining land would be well aware, of course, that in order for you to expand, you would have to buy his land and no other, and he would be likely to hold out for a stiff price, human nature being what it is. In addition, if you buy sufficient land you will insure privacy for yourself and family, even if the surrounding area doesn't develop quite as you had hoped it might. Extra land could provide the opportunity for putting up a cottage and renting it or any number of other possibilities.

Assuming that your locality would make for an attractive vacation spot, this might very well prove a more profitable investment for you than any cash crop you might consider. Given enough land, such a cottage wouldn't necessarily interfere with your privacy in any way. Moreover, with the trend away from the big cities taking on such momentum now, you might be able some day to sell off your extra acres at a neat profit again, provided that the taxes on the extra land weren't too high.

ACREAGE FRONTAGE

Road frontage is important in the country as well as the city, though for somewhat different reasons. The more road frontage a farmer has, the easier it is for him to get to one end of his property or the other without driving his tractor through his own fields or along roads which he might have to build himself. The frontage of the smallest acreage which you buy in the country will probably range from 100 to 300 feet on the road.

Very often, however, you will find that country land is irregular in outline. Given a fairly good road frontage —even a minimum of 100 feet—it might be economical to buy enough back acreage to give you a rectangular piece of property. As a rule acreage off the road is quite a bit cheaper, and you may be able to buy one or two—even more—"back acres" at a considerably lower price than the front acres. Try to avoid buying a triangular piece of property, as the apex of the triangle is difficult to use as a garden, and would be difficult to mow if used for a hayfield.

You may, perhaps, be offered a piece of property having land on both sides of the road. While this is desirable for the commercial farmer who thus has readier access to his fields from the road, and may offer advantages in the way of good roadside stand locations, it presents a problem insofar as his cattle are concerned, if he must cross the road to reach his pasture. Driving cattle across the road to their barns represents a real hazard. If it is a heavily traveled road, the hazard to young children must receive very serious consideration.

Don't expect a farmer or owner of country property to know exactly how many acres of land in each of the fields he has for sale. Most likely he will just approximate it. That is why so many deeds add the words "more or less" to their enumeration of the number of acres. Original surveys rarely were measured in accordance with our more modern scientific methods of surveying. They were likely to be based on natural objects, and sometimes on man-made structures. A description of property might read somewhat like this: "Extending from stone wall on property of Elijah Jones, 200 yards east to property of Seth Brown, then 55 yards to intersection of Middlebury Road, then south to stone wall." Over the years the Jones' property may have been sold again and again, and the name itself might have disappeared; the stone wall may have long since been carted away; the brook diverted, and the Middlebury Road may have been moved back a quarter of a mile.

And farmers especially have been notoriously inexact in their disposal of land over the years. When you ask a farmer how many acres he has for sale, he will have to do a deal of thinking if you try to pin him down. His response may go something like this: "Well, the old place was about 200 acres, I reckon. Then Grandpa turned over around 20 to Pa. Pa sold five acres over on the Ridge, but he bought Uncle Bill's acres on t'other side. That made—let's see—well, anyway, when I took over the place I took what was left of Pa's land, but I bought those five upland acres, so I guess that would leave—maybe about ten acres right here—more or less." But there is a note of optimism here. You are likely to get *more* than less, because country property owners often underestimated the number of their acres.

LOCATION OF LAND

The first thing that may impress itself on you about a piece of land or country property is its location. Land may be bought on top of a hill, at the foot of a hill, or simply on the level. The preferences of people vary, some preferring a location on top of a hill, or at least a hillside, so as to afford a broad view and plenty of sun. Others prefer the woods at the foothills, or the valley. All locations have both their advantages and disadvantages. The hilltop gets the summer breeze, but it also gets winter blasts, making houses built on hilltops harder to heat. Roads leading to the hilltop wash down in heavy rains, and are not easy to negotiate in ice and snow. Soil, too, is washed away by rains.

Property in the valley has a more limited view, but is protected from winter winds. The soil is better generally, and there is usually more shade. Such property may get a good deal of drainage water; perhaps actual flood condition, especially in many parts of New England and the Middle West. Many a person has bought property at "bargain prices," oblivious of the fact that the area was subject to floods whenever creeks or rivers became swollen. Frost conditions tend to be worse in the valleys.

Selecting your location, then, will be a matter of personal preference entirely. A compromise between the two extremes—neither the top of the hill nor the valley—might offer advantages. Various factors enter into a decision as to a desirable location. Proximity to the roads and the town may be deciding factors. Main and secondary roads generally follow the valleys. Farm and wood roads wander up the hills. If you are interested in buying land only, your choice of location is very wide indeed. It becomes a little more limited when you are seeking land with an existing house. With such properties you will find that some thought had been given to the selection of that particular piece of land. Selection of a site for your land becomes, as you see, a more important matter for consideration than would seem apparent on the surface.

THE LAND ITSELF

A study of the topography of any land you are considering is another of the factors demanding a good deal of thought. It is important for two reasons. It may affect your plans for the development of the land, and influence your ultimate costs. You don't need to be told that a hilly, rocky piece of land, while attractive from an artistic point of view, would be of little use as a homestead or a part-time or commercial farm. It is obvious, too, that land that doesn't have a foot of level ground is going to pose all kinds of building problems, even if you had no intention of planting much on it.

Let us consider first the question of the land in relation to the house you plan to put up. The best location for your house is, of course, a fairly level spot. This involves the least amount of labor and would cost the least to develop. Of course, this doesn't offer as attractive a setting for your house as building it on a slight

In choosing a site for a house, or grading the site, a gentle slope away from the house in all directions is preferable. A position at the bottom of a slope or grade is poor because of the likelihood of water trouble in the basement.

rise. As a matter of fact when a cellar is excavated the earth is generally used to give the house a rise from the road.

Perhaps you may be attracted to land which slopes *downward* from the road. Such a site can be used for building and might lend itself to an attractive setting, but it is quite a challenge to the builder. Land of this kind can be utilized only when it *continues* to slope. To build a house at the bottom of a slope would be a sure guarantee of flooding and poor drainage. Generally, steep slopes require retaining walls and terraces, and are expensive to handle. Vacation homes or summer cottages perched on the edge of a hill or over a brook may be lovely and picturesque, but as year-round homes or productive homesteads they are quite out of the question.

Speaking of slopes, you will not have lived long in some parts of the country before you become aware of "established grades." Each village sets up what is known as established grades for its roads and streets. These grades represent the height above sea level. In consider-

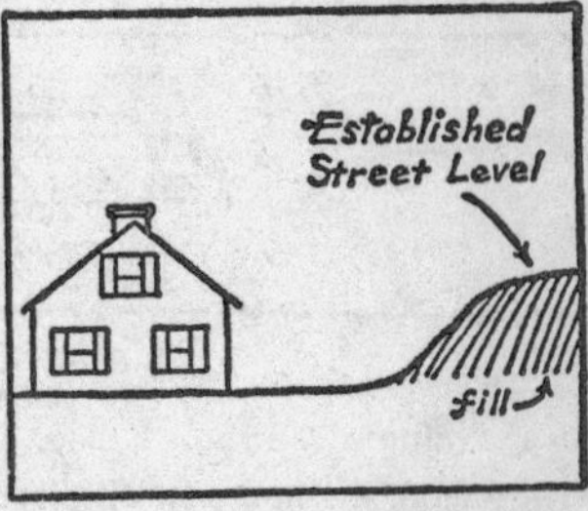

Most communities have "established grades" or street levels but streets as existing may not be at the "established" level. A grading of the street upward to the established level is usually unfortunate for the home owner.

ing country property it is most important to find out whether the road on which your property will be located is at the established grade. The grade determines the height at which a road is supposed to have been built. It may be that the road fronting your property is at the established grade. Quite often, however, you will find that it isn't. If at some future time the "city fathers" decide to grade the road to conform to the established grade, you may suddenly find the road in front of your property being raised. The road will then become accessible to you only by means of a steep roadway—not to mention the fact that your view will be cut off and that traffic henceforth will be above you. Or, if your property should be above the established grade, the road may be lowered, and you will, find yourself with a steep driveway down to the road—not quite as bad as the reverse, to be sure. Should the road be paved, however, you can pretty much assume, then, that the grade has been established. It would be a good idea, if you purchase your land a mile or more beyond where the paving ends, to determine whether the road is at the established grade. Your survey, if you have one, should indicate it.

SURFACE WATER

Surface water is a very important consideration to the country dweller. Surface water is the water which comes to your property from rain, thaws, springs, etc. It may take several forms—either of water left on the land following rain, snow, or thaw, or it may be permanent, as in the case of springs or marshes.

As a rule, the more surface water you have, and the nearer it is to the surface, the more trouble you are going to experience—for surface water does cause trouble. You will have to build your basement floors at least four feet above the highest level of surface water. This is of particular importance in the level portions of the Middle West. Modern builders believe that they can obviate surface water by omitting cellars entirely in new houses. To these builders the cellar is merely a relic of the old gravity heating systems of our fathers. Modern heating systems permit the heating unit to be placed on the ground floor level. It is quite probable, however, that if you buy a country house it will have a cellar. Be on the alert, then, for surface water.

Another problem with surface water will be its effect on your septic system. Local health codes may require you to put in an elaborate, and expensive, system, if there is too much surface water. Worse yet, your land could be declared unfit for building.

If you don't ascertain the presence of surface water before you have made your purchase, you are almost certain to have trouble if you discover it after the property has been bought. Surface water may seep into your cellar. Even if you succeed in pumping it out, it will mean a continuously wet basement. And even if the portion of your land designated for the house has no surface water, scan the rest of your land for evidences of it. Surface water makes most land unusable. To be sure land can be drained, but it is an expensive proposition and hardly pays the average homesteader. Where only a small, restricted area of your land has surface water or is marshy, it may be excavated and made into a fish pond.

There are several ways of finding out whether a piece of land has surface water. Houses in the immediate neighborhood on approximately the same level will show indications of it, and you may ask the owners about it. If you have any doubts about the presence of surface water, tests by an engineer should very definitely be made.

A brook is something else again. A brook adds landscaping value to your property, in addition to providing recreation and sport. For the part-time or full-time farmer a brook means a wonderful watering place for livestock. If it doesn't dry up in summer, it can be used for irrigation. If the land is so located that you could

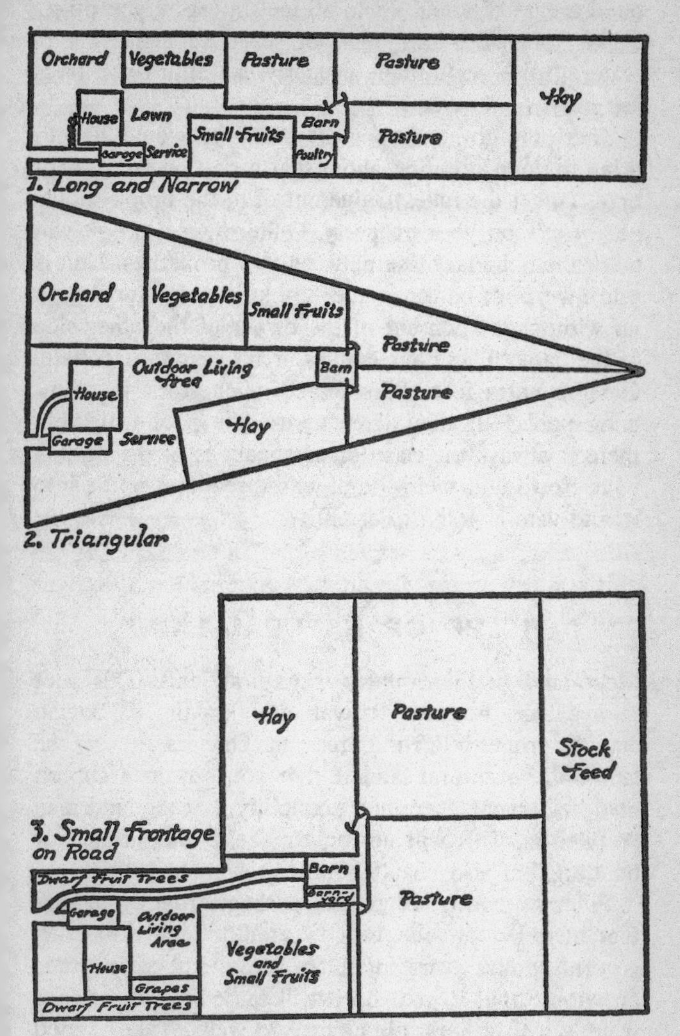

Suggested layouts for odd-shaped land areas.

build a dam of about 25 to 30 feet in width, you might make yourself a fish pond of seven or eight feet of water. A fish pond made properly can afford you fresh fish most of the year.

There is another important point we would like to bring to your attention about that brook on your property. To get the fullest value out of it, the brook should be *entirely* on your property. Quite often a brook will mark the boundary line between two properties. Unless you own both banks of the brook, you cannot dam it up without the consent of the owner of the other side of the bank. These agreements aren't easy to negotiate. Older country folks "don't take much stock in swimming pools." If they agree to use the pool with you, there is always the clash of personalities at the pool—your crowd and theirs—and who threw that bottle into it, and who is going to clean it?

FILLED OR NATURAL LAND

Most land in the country is natural land. This isn't always true, however. If you are thinking of buying country property in rural areas, the chances are that the land will be natural land. But if you buy in a suburb or development, there is a possibility that the land may be filled in. This will not only make it undesirable for building, but also unsuitable for growing anything.

Fill may consist of refuse, garbage, rocks, soil—in fact anything anyone ever wanted to get rid of. It generally takes years for fill to settle, and as it settles any house that is built on it will settle with it, causing trouble with cellars, plumbing and walls. Take a good look at the land. If there are large old trees with their primary roots visible, you can take it for granted that the land in the area hasn't been filled.

If there is any question in your mind as to whether the land has been filled, get the owner's consent to dig a "test pit." This is merely a pit dug to a depth of six or more feet—at which depth you should be able to determine whether the land is filled or not by the presence of ashes, cans, metal, rocks, etc.

Natural ground is, of course, the best ground on which to build. There is, however, one more test you can make if you want to avoid expense in building later on. That is the presence of too much rock. If you find that there is too much rock under the site for which you plan your house, you are going to have to pay for extra excavation and blasting, unless you omit the cellar, as suggested previously. If you see boulders or outcroppings of rock, that is pretty good evidence of the fact that the rocks may get more numerous as you dig down.

If the site you have chosen for your house contains a few large, old, graceful trees, you will want to keep as many of them as you can. Dead trees or stumps should, of course, be removed. It will involve a considerable bit of expense.

There is a good deal of variation in soil quality, too, and you should give some attention to the soil in planning your house. Silt, which is finely divided ordinary soil, makes a very poor foundation. Gravel and clay are the best types of soil on which to build.

GOOD OR POOR LAND?

To those of us who plan a homestead, the land ought to have one other desirable quality—it must be fertile and productive. You can make poor land more or less productive with topsoil, fertilizer, manure or "green manure," and hard work but this is expensive and time-consuming. It can set back the full productive possibilities of your homestead by several years. Therefore, those who are planning on a fully productive homestead should give as much—if not *more*—consideration to the productivity of the land as to the adaptability of the house. A good farmer gives primary consideration to the land; a good point to remember.

When you realize that ponderous volumes have been written on the soil, its function, its fertility, its reclamation—you may understand the difficulty of giving you enough information in these few pages to make you even an amateur judge of soil and land. We hope, in all earnestness, that if you are planning any kind of farming, or even a homestead, you will study the soil.

However, there are several simple indications of soil fertility which may be of help to you. The local library will have government soil maps, or they can be secured from the Department of Agriculture in Washington. These should give you some helpful information regarding the soil in your area. If there is a farmer or someone with a garden next door, he may be able to give you sound advice on the general fertility of the soil in the immediate neighborhood.

Certain trees indicate certain types of soil. For example, beech, sugar-maple, white oak and black walnut trees almost invariably indicate good ground. White pine, scrub oak and scrawny trees in general mean poor ground. Full-grown willows, poplars and alders generally mean too much water in the soil.

Notice the weeds which the soil supports. Contrary to popular opinion, a good crop of weeds usually indicates good soil. If the weeds are dark-green, abundant and sturdy, the soil is probably good. If the weeds are straggling and pale, or if there are frequent bare spots in the fields, then you can be pretty sure the soil isn't worth much. While ox-eyed daisies are pretty, their presence in a field shows lack of humus or leaf-mold, as do wild carrots or mullein. In general, if land can't support such hardy plants as weeds, it won't support a good crop. And another thing: don't judge ground after a rain! Even poor ground looks fairly good when wet. It is much better to look at the ground during a dry spell.

Pick up some soil. Roll it into a ball. Smell it. Notice whether it hardens into a lump of mud, or remains light and friable, crumbling easily!

There are soil-testing kits on the market which enable you to test the soil on any land you are considering. The value of these soil kits as final arbiters is very much open to question. If you had the time to learn a few things about hunger signs in plants, you probably could detect the absence of many soil elements in the property you looked at. In the absence of this knowledge, much sounder judgments are possible through weeds as indicators, and the appearance of plants already on the property.

You can also submit soil samples from various parts of the land you are interested in to the agricultural experiment station of your state. Soil is tested either free, or at a very nominal cost. Dig several test holes to examine the depth of the topsoil. They should be at least 7 inches deep—12 inches might be better. If the topsoil is only 6 or 7 inches deep, it should at least rest on fairly good clay. If it rests on hard-pan or deep gravel, all indications would point to the fact that you are going to have trouble with it, and you should consider twice before buying.

CONDITION OF THE LAND

Look closely at the condition of the land. If it is covered with rocks, stones, outcroppings of boulders, underbrush of over 6 inches in diameter, or tree stumps, it is going to cost money to clear it. It is costly to uproot even small trees and stumps, let alone clearing it for cultivation. If there are stumps on the land, look at them. If they are stumps of the white pine, white oak, cedar or locust trees, they are going to be hard to remove, because these woods don't decay rapidly. If the stumps are of maple, cottonwood, ash and varieties of the pine other than the above, these stumps could be removed more easily as the wood of these stumps decays more rapidly.

Notice whether there is timber on the land you are buying. Wood lots are a valuable source of firewood and fence posts. In property far enough away from cities many pieces of land have good timber value on them, although it may take a professional forester to estimate its worth. But take the word of such an expert *only,* and not that of a real estate broker or other amateur who may point out to you that there is valuable timber on the land which will help you to pay for the property. Unless the timber is of sizable amount and dimension, there is little profit in small timber land. Clear only those trees on your land that are past their prime. Never denude your land of timber even though you might show a temporary profit.

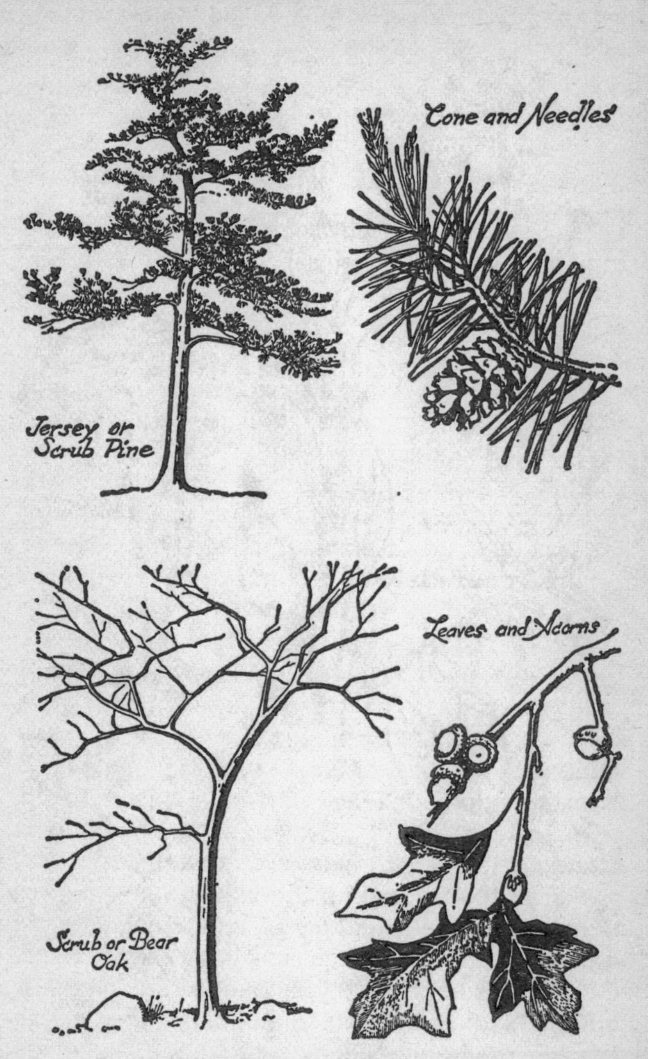

These trees often indicate poor soil.

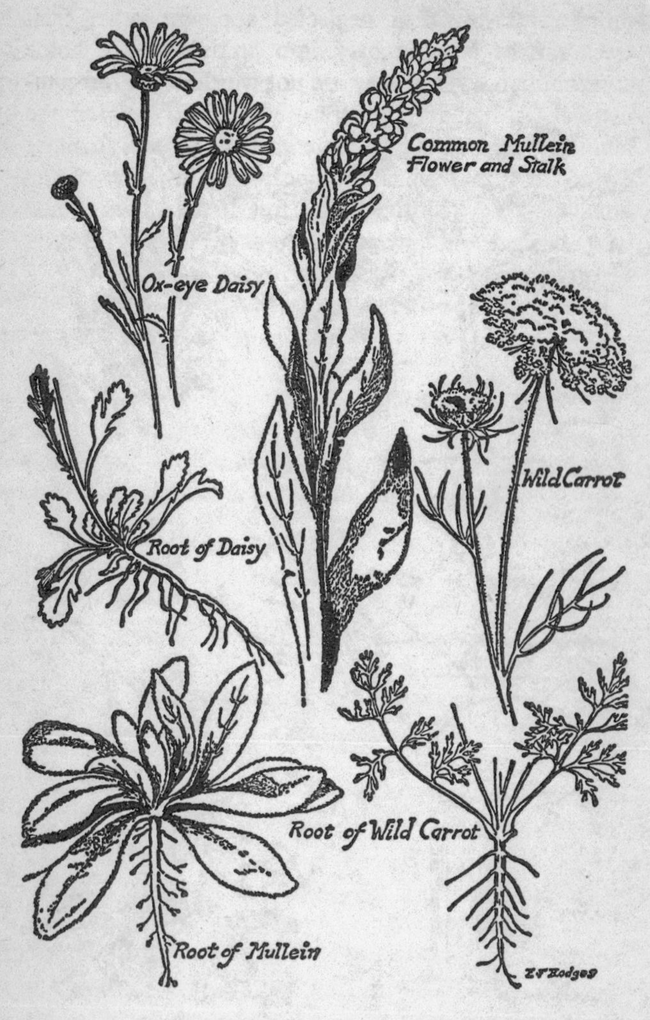

One or more of these weeds are usually found where soil is poor.

Orchard or fruit trees on the land make it that much more valuable. Often neglected apple or other fruit trees can be brought back into production for home consumption, even if they are not worth much for commercial production. If there are no fruit trees on the land, it is interesting to remember that you can plant dwarf fruit trees which will bear in a fraction of the time it takes a full-sized fruit tree to bear. Of course berry bushes, grape-vines and other perennial plants on the property all add some little value to it.

Chapter Five

HOW TO JUDGE THE TRUE CONDITION OF A HOUSE

Your search for country property, of course, involves either the purchase of an existing house, with land, or a piece of land on which to build a house. This chapter concerns itself with the existing house. In evaluating such a house you are going to be subjected to perhaps the most difficult of all buying tasks.

The casualness with which most of us investigate houses we are considering buying is little short of amazing. What is the usual procedure? You take a look at the living room to ascertain the view, the number of windows, and the size. You cast an appraising eye at the fireplace: decide how you would like to have the room decorated, and that's that. You may be intrigued by the streamlined kitchen, and wonder how it would look with your own kitchen set. Someone reminded you that cross-ventilation is best for a bedroom, so, after you have counted the windows and figured whether the space was large enough for your bedroom furniture, you have checked that room off against your mental list. You take a hasty glance at the attic, look up at the rafters to make sure there are no leaks in the roof, and then make a quick trip to the cellar to poke at the furnace, if there is one. That is the average house search.

There is no reason for such heedlessness. A little information and a few simple tests will give you a fair basis for judging, with some degree of reliability, any house you might consider buying. You won't become an expert appraiser of houses, but at least you will be able to recognize the most obvious defects, omissions and economies, as well as any downright fakes that may have been perpetrated. You will be able to satisfy yourself more assuredly as to whether the house is or isn't worth considering further. Once you have reached that decision, you will have time enough to call in more expert advice. But, as you know, you can't take a builder along with you to every house you look at.

The most important tests are those which will enable you to determine whether a country house is of sound construction, in good condition, and worth considering. Many, if not most, of the houses you will see will require remodeling to a greater or lesser extent. In this chapter, however, we shall confine ourselves primarily to a consideration of the older, well-built type of house, such as will require little major remodeling.

These older houses are likely to be your best buy in the country because of their good construction, but lack the expensive, modern conveniences that you can add later, such as extra baths and fancy kitchens. Newer

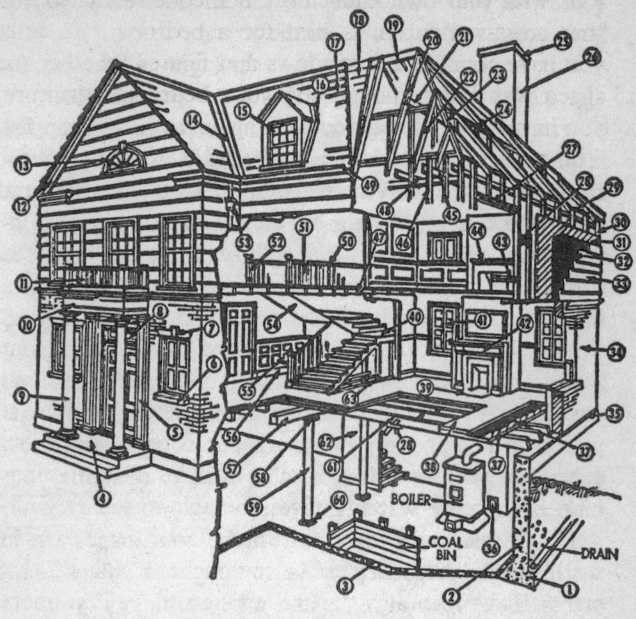

63 items to check in buying a house

1. Footing.
2. Foundation wall.
3. Basement floor.
4. Porch floor.
5. Pilaster.
6. Window sill.
7. Key stone.
8. Transom.
9. Column.
10. Entablature.
11. Balustrade.
12. Cornice.
13. Fan window.
14. Valley.
15. Dormer window.
16. Flashing.
17. Shingles.
18. Roof sheathing.
19. Ridge.
20. Common rafter.
21. Collar beam.
22. Jack rafter.
23. Hip rafter.
24. Purlin.
25. Chimney cap.
26. Chimney.
27. Header.
28. Bridging.
29. Plate.
30. Corner post.
31. Sheathing.
32. Building paper.
33. Siding.
34. Brick.
35. Water table.
36. Cleanout door.
37. Subfloor.
38. Finish floor.
39. Hearth.
40. Stair landing.
41. Casement window.
42. Fire place.
43. Rough sill.
44. Mantle.
45. Ceiling joists.
46. Studding.
47. Floor joists.
48. Ribbon.
49. Gutter.
50. Handrail.
51. Balustrade.
52. Newel.
53. Leader head.
54. Stair soffit.
55. Wainscoting.
56. Base.
57. Girder.
58. Column cap.
59. Basement column.
60. Column base.
61. Joist.
62. Partition.
63. Lath.

homes, if well built, may be too expensive; if poorly built you are better off avoiding them.

It is impossible to "take in" thoroughly all the details of a house the first time you see it. You wouldn't, of course, subject the owners of a house to such intensive inspection unless you found the major aspects of construction reasonably satisfactory, as the inspection would necessitate quite a bit of "snooping" and knocking about. No doubt the majority of houses you see will be occupied. Some owners will give you carte blanche to go anywhere you choose in the house, and will leave you alone. Others, however, will hover about anxiously, offering help and explanations and distracting you from your purpose of an intensive inspection. If you cannot gracefully evade their accompanying presence, you have no recourse other than to continue your task under their watchful eyes.

If it is necessary for you to make your inspection in the owner's presence, avoid making too many comments. Take mental notes and a few jottings if you can do so unobtrusively. Ask questions concerning the points brought up in this chapter, doing it as carefully as you can without antagonizing the owner in the process. Take plenty of time and look at the house from basement to attic—in fact *concentrate* on the basement and attic, as it is there that you will find the key to the basic construction of the house.

In looking at a house, make a simple sketch of the floor plan and outside appearance. If you are sufficiently interested, and have a camera along, take a picture of the exterior. Note the conditions you have found on the sketch you have drawn, in accordance with the recommendations made in this chapter. Incidentally, if you are able to get the name of the contractor who built the house, he might be willing to show you the original specifications. If they are made available to you, they will tell you far more about the house than the most intensive kind of personal investigation you can make.

LOOK AT THE BASEMENT

The basement is important for two reasons. It will give you the opportunity for judging the soundness of the house construction, and for judging the walls which hold up the house. In many country houses the basement extends under only part of the house, the rest being only slightly excavated, leaving but a foot or two of space under which drain and supply pipes may run. All unexcavated areas of the basement should be at least 2½ feet in height between the ground and the floor, so that repairs can be made easily. The basement itself should be at least 6 to 7 feet high.

Being the lowest part of the house, rain and ground or surface water are likely to drain into the basement. There should be a water drain in the lowest part of the basement floor—unless the house is located in a hollow. You will have no trouble recognizing the cast-iron drain grating. Such a drain leads either to the sewer, if there is one, to a dry well, or cesspool. Generally cellars drain by gravity, but in a habitually wet cellar it must be pumped out by means of a sump pump. If you see such a pump in the cellar, it means that the house suffers chronically from wet cellars. You can tell whether a basement drain is working by pouring a little water into it. If it drains well the water will flow down easily and quickly. Usually the floor drain will lead off to a stone filled pit, but it is most desirable to have the drainage pipe lead off to an exposed outlet. In newer homes a properly installed perimeter drainage system will help to keep the cellar dry. In some cases the installation of such a perimeter drainage system around an old house will be helpful, but it is apt to be quite costly as a good deal of hand labor is involved. If such a system is installed, every effort should be made to have the lead-off pipe run out to an exposed outlet. On the market today there are many waterproofing sealants that are available, that work with varying degrees of success, when applied to the inside of a block or poured concrete cellar wall.

Look at the basement walls. If you should see a line running anywhere from an inch to about six inches around the walls over the floor, the probability is that it is a waterline, and means that the cellar has been flooded to that height. If the cellar is dark, smells damp, and is built of stone in which you see many crevices or holes, you can be pretty sure you have a cellar that is going to give you trouble. If the cellar floor is made of concrete, it would be a good idea to test its thickness. Some concrete floors are built on a very thin base of cinders, and if this base is *too* thin, water may get under the basement floor and cause it to crack. Sometimes, too, the fill settles and leaves an open space between the cinders and the concrete. If this is true you have another situation in which water may get under the floor. You can test the solidity of the floor by tapping various parts of it with a hammer. If the sound is flat or dull, the floor is probably solid. If the sound changes to a thin or hollow one, then either the concrete is too thin, or the fill has settled. On the other hand, if the cellar walls are of concrete, are even, have no cracks, and if the floor and walls are dry, you may be sure you have a pretty good cellar.

Houses stand on what are known as "footings." These are masonry slabs which hold up the foundation walls. You can't see them when the house is finished as they are concealed, the walls having been built on them. But if you should notice some vertical, open cracks in the foundation, whether on the inside or outside, this is evidence that either the footings have settled, are weak, or even there may be *no* footings!

The foundation is built on the footings. Several types of masonry may be used for the foundation—stone, brick, poured concrete, cinder blocks, etc. If the basement wall has been built of concrete blocks, note whether there are any vertical cracks in the joints between the blocks. This is generally due to unstable ground beneath the foundation footings. Little can be done about it, except to keep an eye on the condition. If the foundation is full of holes, it will need "pointing up," that is, the holes will have to be filled with mortar or otherwise repaired.

The "frame" of the house rests on the foundation. A house is "framed" by a fairly intricate system of joists, girders, studs, bridging, posts and walls, but it won't be necessary to go into the details of such construction now. What you are primarily interested in on this initial inspection is the condition of the *lumber* in the frame of the house.

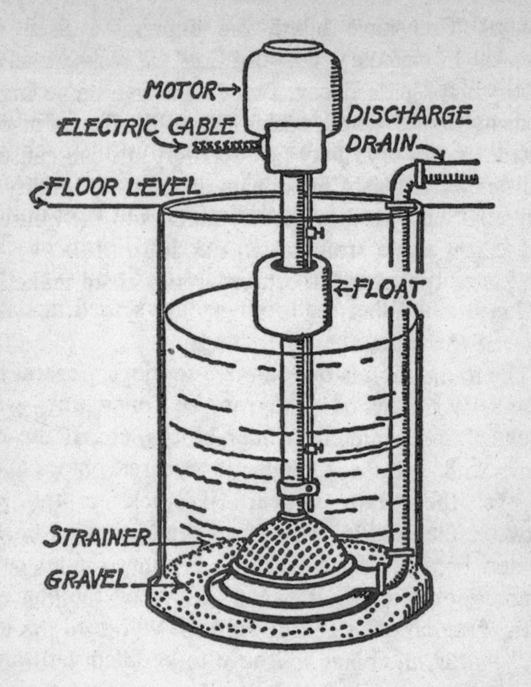

Presence of a sump pump, illustrated above, in a cellar is a sign that water is a problem, although the pump may take care of the seepage satisfactorily.

BEWARE OF DRY ROT

In the upper rooms of an older house the lumber is covered with lath and plaster. It is only in the cellar and attic that the lumber is exposed. Either will give you an opportunity to look into a condition known as "dry rot"—a condition frequently found in old country houses. You have heard the expression used often enough in ordinary conversation to know that it is synonymous with decay. Dry rot, as the name implies, is decay of the wood, which sets in to the point of reducing it to a dry, flaky powder! Dry rot can cause any amount of anguish, for it eats at the very vitality of a house. It can run through key timbers in the house and cause the whole structure to sag and buckle.

One of the most important tests of all to make is for dry rot. If this condition is present, you will detect it most easily at the point where the wood of the house rests on the masonry foundations. Stick a sharp knife blade into the wood at that point. If the blade goes in "hard," and is difficult to remove, chances are the lumber is sound. If it goes in easily and comes out just as easily, with a film of brown powder on it, dry rot very likely is present. To be sure, dry rot may be present to some extent in any wood-timbered house. If your knife blade doesn't go in beyond, say, three-eighths of an inch, there may be decades of life still left in the wood, especially if the result is the same after you test a dozen or more spots. Another test for dry rot is to observe the floor for signs of reddish dust or powder. This represents a very active stage of deterioration and is a bad sign indeed. You had better forget all about the place, then, and go on to the next!

Now, look at the beams supporting the first floor. Are they true and firm? If they are, then there is probably good lumber and workmanship in the house. But if the timbers still have bark on them, if you notice broken joints and large knots, then you may be sure you have poor lumber and poorer work. This is more true of houses that have been built within the past hundred years. It was quite customary, in old Colonial houses, to use half-hewn floor beams with the bark retained on them. There are innumerable sound old houses of this kind with the bark still on the beams. It won't be difficult for you to recognize the enormous, hand-hewn framework of such old houses, and they are probably good for many more years! We are talking now primarily of comparatively modern houses with poor timbers. In newer construction in which dimensional lumber has been used, a good indication of sound construction will be the presence of bridging—i.e., wood or metal pieces that are placed between the floor joists to keep them from warping. And if lumber and workmanship are poor in the cellar where anyone can see it, you may be sure that they are still poorer upstairs, where they are hidden!

THE HEATING SYSTEM

If the house you are considering has central heating, check the heating system. We won't go into the question of the various types of heating plants. Hours may be spent by home owners defending their particular type of heating system. All you want to know is whether the heating system keeps the house warm. You can, of course, ask the owner, but we can't imagine the owner trying to sell a house confessing to you that his family nearly froze to death last winter.

If you were a heating engineer, you would be at an advantage in judging the heating system, of course. Remember that a good deal of the efficiency of the system will depend on the soundness of the whole house, the insulation plus good planning for whatever type of heating system is used. If the house isn't sound and has *no* insulation, the chances that the system will deliver enough heat are slight. Here is a tip. If you visit the house during the winter or early spring, and find that several rooms have been "cut off," you can be fairly certain that they were cut off to conserve heat, and that the system cannot heat the entire house. Of course this interpretation of the "cut-off" rooms doesn't hold in every situation. Sometimes the house is too large for present family needs, and so thrifty people resort to this to conserve fuel.

If the system uses gas or oil, you might find out where the owner gets his fuel by casually asking whether there is a nearby dependable source of supply. The company might tell you whether the system burns up an inordinate amount of fuel. However, the fuel man's first loyalty is to his present customer, and, besides, the poorer the system, the more fuel used, which is where the fuel man's interest lies. But if you are seriously concerned about the system, it would be desirable to have it looked at by an impartial heating man.

If there is central heating, there may be a hot water system in the cellar, too. There are two ways of securing hot water—either in connection with the heating system, or as a separate unit. Look at the hot water tank. The effectiveness of the tank depends both on capacity and water temperature. Usually the capacity is printed on the tank, but if the tank is old, or painted over, take note of its dimensions. It should be about five feet long and about two feet in diameter. If the tank is smaller, in all probability there won't be enough hot water to go around for the average family accustomed to city conveniences.

THE PLUMBING SYSTEM

As in the case of heating, we hardly expect you to become a plumbing expert over night. That is best left to the local plumber. There are a few things that you might observe in the cellar, however, which might furnish a few clues as to whether the plumbing is good or bad. You will notice two kinds of plumbing pipes. The large ones are drain pipes. Obviously as these drain the waste from the kitchen and bathroom, they are necessarily large. They are usually made of iron. In new, cheaper construction plastic drain pipes are sometimes being used, if the local building code allows it. If properly installed this can be satisfactory pipe, but is obviously not as sturdy as the cast iron.

You will see smaller pipes, also, called supply pipes, because they supply water. They are smaller because the water moves through them faster since it is under pressure. Supply pipes usually are made of copper. Manufacturers contend that these metals last longer and do not discolor the water, but they do, undeniably, corrode under certain water conditions. Genuine wrought iron supply pipes, as used in older construction, have stood up very well, as many house owners can testify. Because these pipes deliver the water you drink, they naturally wouldn't be made of iron that rusts or discolors the water, in addition to corroding and springing leaks.

Supply pipes in new, good construction jobs are made of copper. Just a few scratches with your pen-knife on the supply pipes will show the metal of which they are made. Copper will shine, while iron pipes remain dull. As a rule ordinary iron pipes indicate a cheap plumbing job.

Look at both drainage and supply pipes in various parts of the cellar for what are known as "plugs." You will find them where the pipes turn a corner or change their direction. Such points are likely to become clogged with waste. These plugs can be opened and the waste removed. If you don't see at least one or two plugs, you can be sure the plumbing job is a skimpy one, and you can also expect plumbing bills when the pipes do become clogged.

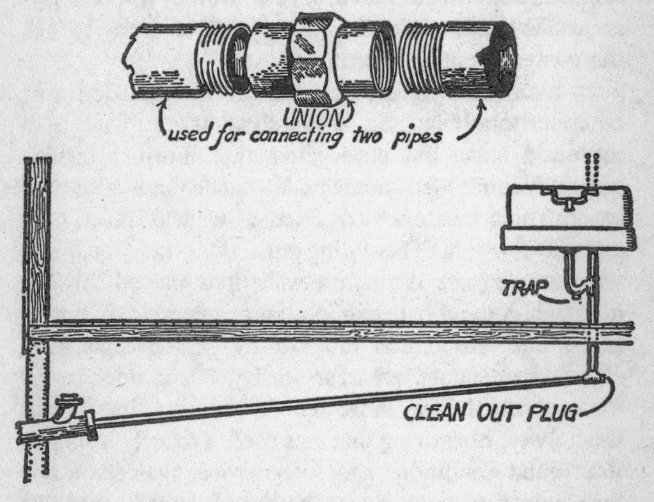

Unions and plugs in the plumbing facilitate cleaning and repair of the system.

One of the most important parts of the pipe system is the presence of "unions," so that the installation can be opened up readily for repairs and alterations.

THE ELECTRIC SYSTEM

Parts of the electric system are left exposed, also, in the cellar, so that you can get some idea at least of the workmanship. You probably do not know enough about electrical installations to judge as to whether the system is good or bad. The inspection of electrical work required by most communities for both new and remodeled houses may offer you some protection. When such inspection is required, a certificate of inspection is issued. If you are interested in buying the property, ask the owner about the certificate.

In many country districts, however, inspection may be either totally lacking or slip-shod. It may have been inspected once, but never after that. Former owners may have installed homemade, inadequate electrical work. These jobs once consisted of what is called tube and knob wiring. The wiring runs along the walls, and whenever it goes through a wall, it is passed through a porcelain tube, being supported at intervals by porcelain knobs. Knob and tube wiring isn't necessarily a sign of inadequate, amateur wiring, but it does reveal the *age* of a house, more or less. At one time it was the only type of wiring that was used. Properly installed, if in good condition, and safeguarded against outside mechanical damage, it may be better, in fact, than the convenient, newer BX wiring that often corrodes in damp places. In the BX system the electric wires are led through flexible, metal tubing. If the house has this type of wiring you would be advised to call in an electrician to estimate how much it will cost to put in adequate modern wiring consisting of plastic-coated wire with proper grounding.

FIREPLACES

If the house has a fireplace, it is supported on the foundations of the house, or else on a separate foundation. Make sure that the support is not sagging. If the support is of wood, be sure there is plenty of masonry over it. Modern fireplaces will have an ash pit either in the cellar or outdoors for the disposal of waste.

While still in the basement, look at the ceiling, which is really the floor of the rooms above. As you will learn, floors consist of several layers, the more the better. If there is only one layer to the first floor you may even be able to see the light from the room above. A single-layer floor would, of course, be a very poor floor.

The stair construction of a house is another one of the things usually concealed when the house is finished. But it is generally exposed in the cellar, so that you have the opportunity to judge as to whether the carpentry work is good and sound. The basement stairs should have a firm, strong rail, and should be neither too narrow nor too steep.

You have now made a pretty thorough inspection of the basement, and you are ready to go upstairs. Again let us remind you that we are not concerned now with the plan of the house, but solely with the actual physical construction. The plan of the rooms, orientation and decoration are things you will have to determine for yourself, based on your individual needs and inclinations.

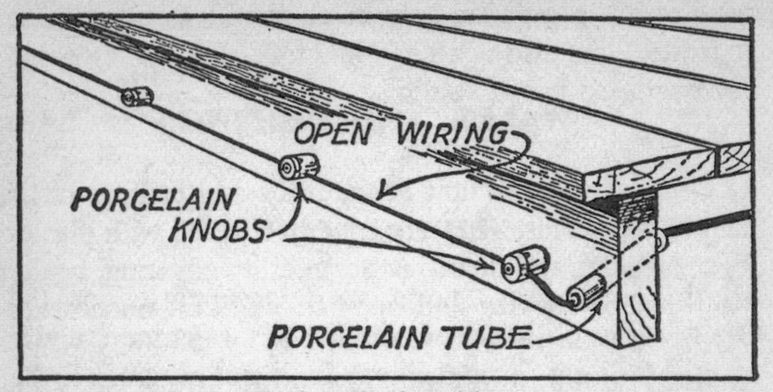

Knob and tube wiring.

Bx cable in use in house wiring.

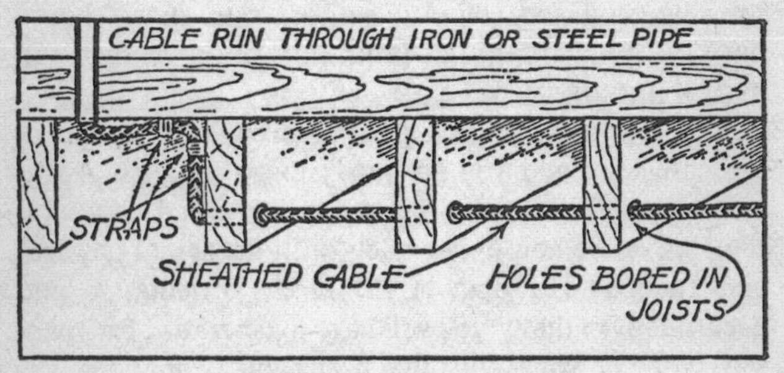

Sheathed cable type of wiring.

WALLS AND CEILINGS

Let us take a look now at the walls and ceilings of the first floor rooms. They are usually covered with plaster, paper, paint, wallboard, or some other covering, so that it won't be easy to find out the condition underneath. However, look a little more closely at the ceilings and walls. Are they level and true, or do they "wave"? Get close up to several walls and squint along them with one eye. If the wall is wavy or untrue, you will notice it. This means one or more of several things—poor workmanship, poor materials, or settling; in short, it isn't good! If there is a fireplace in the living room, notice whether there are any cracks spreading out of the corners of the chimney. This invariably means settling. In looking at a brick house, make sure that the plaster hasn't been applied directly to the brick, but has been attached by lath. Brick walls without laths are called "unfurred walls," and such walls "sweat," causing cracks and poor ventilation in the room.

If the walls are covered with paint, kalsomine, or other thin material, try to see whether the plaster is broken, chipped, or cracked. Poor walls are often covered with attractive wallpaper. This is a favorite trick of the wise builder, remodeler, and even the owner. So don't be misled by fancy wallpapers. Run your hand over the papered wall to see whether the wall is smooth. Tap it to see if the plaster beneath is loose. Look at the corners of the room. It is here that paper usually buckles and cracks. And here is another tip. On good plaster work, what is referred to as a "bead" is attached to the frame at the corners and angles of the room. This is a narrow metal strip which makes the corners firm. If it is covered with plaster or paper so that you can't see it, you can sometimes feel it with your finger-tips, or hear its metallic ring by tapping with a knife or screw driver.

In a remodelled or newer house the walls may be made of sheetrock instead of lath and plaster. If the joints are very obvious under paint or wallpaper, it may indicate poor workmanship. Another popular wall covering is imitation wood panelling. This is all right, if you like the looks of it, (remember it won't mellow with age like real wood), and find by tapping along the wall that it is nailed to enough studs to be solid.

LOOKING AT THE WOODWORK

Now look at the woodwork—called trim by builders. This includes baseboards, molding, and any other wooden coverings. There are two types of wood used in woodwork, hard wood and soft wood. Hard wood is better. Ask what type of wood was used in the trim. If soft wood was used, you are very apt to find dents, hammer marks, scratches and other marrings. If hard wood was used, it will usually be smooth and even, although poor carpenters make dents even in hardwood trims. Look at the joints in door and window construction. If they are true, and not wavy, if they are not filled in or crooked, you can assume that the construction is pretty good.

WINDOWS

Let us look at the windows now. There are three general types of windows in older homes—double hung, fixed sash, and casement. Casement windows, as you probably know, have hinges at the side and open outward. Fixed-sash windows provide light, but were never intended to be opened. Double-hung windows are the windows found in most houses, with the upper part sliding down and the lower part sliding up. They are balanced by sash weights. Old houses in the country are likely not to have sash weights, the lower part merely sliding up, and having permanent springs in the window sash which plunge into holes bored into the frame. They may be picturesque, but not very satisfactory. Cheap windows are also indicated by their lack of lifts and window locks.

THE FLOORS

A floor generally consists of three layers. The lowest layer is called a sub-floor, and is nailed diagonally or at right angles to the joists which hold the entire floor up. The boards in the sub-floor should be at least 1 inch thick by 4 inches wide You can note this from the cellar. Heavy building paper, acting as a cushion and insulation, is placed over the sub-floor. Above this paper is laid the floor as you see it. This top layer of floor may be made either of soft or hard wood, the latter, of course, being the more desirable. As important as the

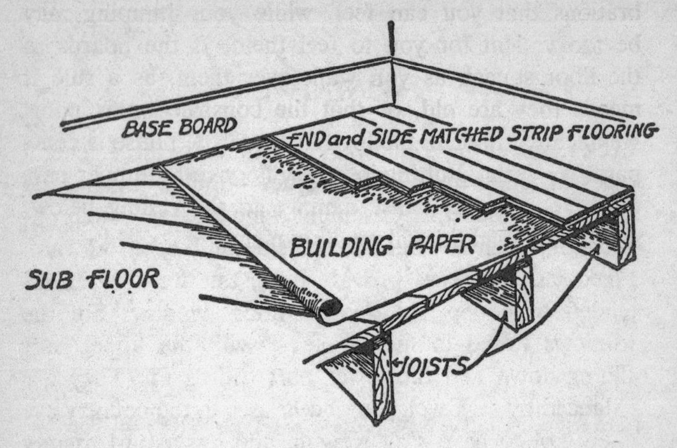

Floor construction.

wood, however, is the condition which the floor is in.

Are the floors level, or do they sag? If they sag it may mean one of several things—the wood has shrunk, the house has settled, the construction is weak, or the timbers which hold the floor up are inadequate—all pretty risky. Wide cracks between the floor boards often mean poor construction. Poor floors may be covered with linoleum. If this is done anywhere except in the kitchen, be extra wary. If there is any possibility of doing it, lift up the linoleum and look at the flooring. If you can't lift it up, you may be able to get some idea of the condition of the flooring by pressing your hands on the linoleum to determine whether the floor underneath is firm and level.

Walk on the floors with a firm step. They shouldn't vibrate or shake. Jump up and down lightly—if you dare! If the floor isn't firm, glassware and pictures may rattle. Or, if you prefer a milder test, stand on your toes and jiggle hard. This will set up vibrations that you can feel, while your jumping may be too violent for you to feel them. If the boards in the floor squeak as you walk over them, as a rule it means they are old, or that the construction is poor. Replacing a floor in the lower part of the house is comparatively easy. Putting in a new floor in the upper part of the house may cause damage to the ceiling below, necessitating additional repair expense.

STAIRS

Let us go upstairs, now, and while you are about it, look at the stairs going to the second floor. The part of the step which rises is naturally called the riser, and the step itself is called the tread. In some of the old houses you will often find a lack of comfortable proportion between the riser and the tread. Risers may be too high, which makes for a steep and dangerous stairway. Risers should rarely be more than 7 inches high. Treads should be at least 10 inches wide from riser to riser. As you walk up the stairs, notice whether there is a squeak. A squeak at either the top or the bottom probably means poor stair construction. If the squeak occurs in the middle of the flight, it may mean just a loose tread.

BATHROOM

If the bathroom is upstairs, look at the plumbing. You can generally tell from its style and condition how old it is. Test the water pressure. Open the faucets widely in the bathroom. If the water splashes out in a good stream, the water pressure probably will be adequate. We have a friend who bought a house and later discovered that there wasn't enough water pressure to boost water to an upstairs bath! Let some water run into the washbowl and bathtub. If it runs off quietly and quickly, you can assume the pipes are clear; if not, they may be clogged. This isn't too serious a condition, but enough to warrant your taking a closer look at the plumbing. If the water gurgles as it drains, there may not be enough vents—another indication of short-sighted economy in plumbing.

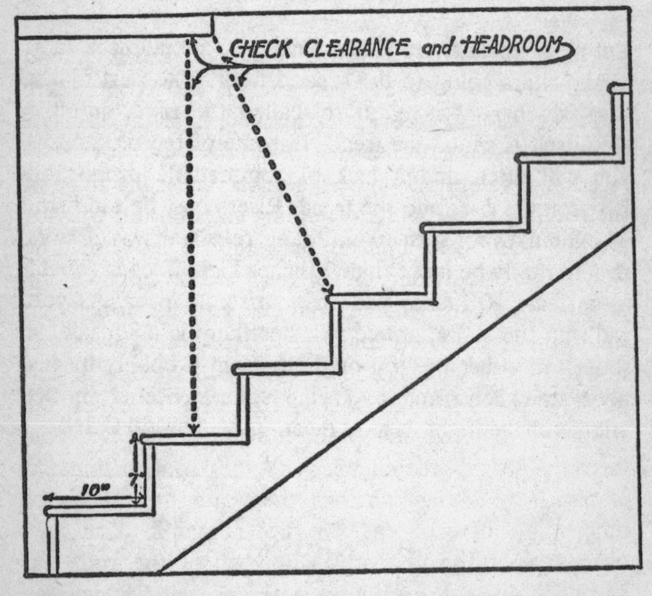

Here are shown good properties of treads and risers in a staircase for safety and comfort. Low headroom may cause painful bumps; low clearance may prevent movement of important items of furniture.

THE ATTIC—ANOTHER IMPORTANT SPOT

Now let us look at the attic. Here, too, the framework of the house is exposed, and that should be another of your primary interests. As you know, the wooden beams which support the roof are the *rafters*. These meet at the highest point of the roof, called the ridge. Rafters should be at least 2 inches thick and 6 inches wide. If they are smaller, you have an example of more misplaced economy Rafters, depending on width, should be from 18 inches to 2 feet apart from the center of one rafter to another Larger spaces again point to poor economy and less roof support.

Look at the point where the rafters meet the ridge of the roof. Are the points of joining smooth and true, or are they reinforced, built up or gaping? They should be well made and strong. Walk over to the edge of the attic floor and see whether you can peer down between the floor and the sloping wall. If the house has been insulated, you will be able to see the insulation at this point. Now look up at the roof to what is called the *sheathing*. This is the wood covering nailed to the rafters on which the shingles or other roofing material is attached. Notice whether there are any stains or other signs of roof-leak on the sheathing. You may observe spots on the attic floor where the roof has leaked. You may even find pots and pans which the occupants forgot to remove, put there to catch the water from the leaks!

Is the attic ventilated, preferably cross-ventilated? It

should be, as otherwise ice may form in the attic by condensation and melt in the spring, leaking to the rooms below If the chimney goes through the attic, notice whether the wood around the chimney is burned or charred, either at the level of the floor or roof. This is a fire hazard. The mortar in the chimney may have lost its strength, in an old house, and there may be holes between the bricks.

THE ROOF

If you can, look at the roof from the attic. If you can't see it from the attic, you may be able to look at it from an upstairs window or from a ladder. Try to get close enough to observe whether the roof covering is good and sound, or whether it is loose, torn, or sagging. Look at the lowest parts of the roof, where the rain water is caught in metal strips called *gutters*. These often rot and leak. Leaky gutters can ruin a good outside or inside wall. Downspouts, which are pipes that lead the water from the gutters to the ground, are also subject to rust.

OUTSIDE WALLS

Let us walk outside next and look at the outside walls. If you are looking at a brick-veneer exterior house wall, see if there are any open horizontal cracks. If the crack runs quite a distance, it may mean that the brick wall is out of plumb, and is tipping outward. This is

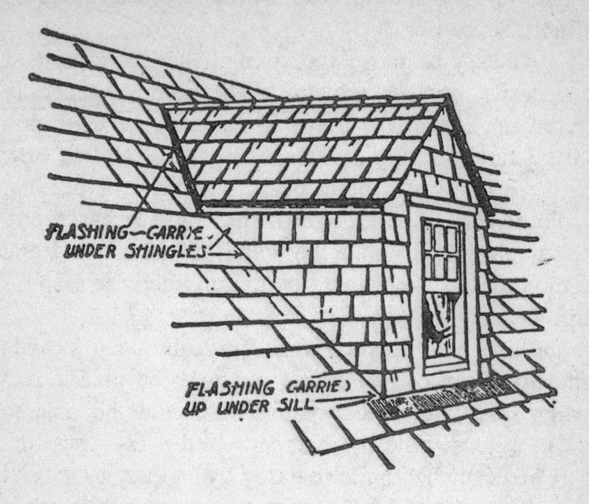

Use of flashing illustrated. Flashings prevent leaks under storm conditions.

not a usual condition, and is a dangerous one. Test the mortar between the bricks with your pocket knife. If it comes off readily in powderlike particles, it is a sign of aging mortar, of course. If it is solid and hard to remove, it is likely that the mortar and brick construction are good

Occasionally in a wooden house of skimpy construction, the outside boards of "siding" are nailed directly on the framework or "studding" with no "sheathing," or what may be called an under layer of boards or plywood nailed on the studding. You can generally tell when this has been done by hitting the siding a good rap with a hammer. A sheathed wall will give off a heavy, solid sound, while a wall without sheathing will sound thin and hollow. If you ever wanted to add shingles to such a wall, you would have considerable additional expenses.

It isn't easy to judge the strength and condition of house walls, because the inside sheathing is generally covered up. But if the house is painted, the condition of the paint job may reveal a good deal. Notice how well the house walls retain paint; whether it is peeling, discolored, full of holes, etc. If the house is part wood and part masonry, notice the points at which wood and masonry meet. They should be tight. Otherwise seepage is apt to cause dry rot.

You have now finished what has really been a quick inspection tour of any house you may be considering buying. We believe that you should now be able to look at a house with more experienced eyes—eyes that won't be bewitched quite so easily by a glossy new paint job, a "streamlined" kitchen, and other neat little tricks that merely dress up a poor house. But there are many details which go into such construction which haven't even been touched upon. And there are exceptions to almost all of the "tests" which have been given in this chapter. What you can depend on is the fact that if your initial inspection has disclosed a great many of the weaknesses pointed out in this chapter, you had better go no farther. If you are undecided as to the desirability of a house, or if you are convinced that the house is a sound one and you are tempted to buy it, call in an architect or builder for advice. We have tried to save you the expense of such a consultation by pointing out the obvious things. But before you act, you will want expert corroboration.

Chapter Six

WHEN IS IT WORTH WHILE TO REMODEL?

In Chapter 5 we guided you through the steps of judging a house which you might consider buying. We assumed that the house as it stood met most of your requirements for modern living, and needed little or no remodeling. We presupposed that no major structural changes or repairs were necessary.

In your search for country property, however, you are going to be shown houses which may, in few senses of the word, be considered modern—houses that it is obvious will require major remodeling and improvement. Present owners are aware of this, and, as a rule, reduce the price of these houses accordingly. "Imagine a ten-room house for only $15,000." "If you figure the land is worth $5,000 alone, the house is practically thrown in." These are the arguments you are going to hear when you start looking at old country houses.

You will recall, also, the stories you have read in "home-building" magazines of the tumble-down old shack which, through the ingenuity and industry of the new owners, was transformed into a picturesque, comfortable home at practically no cost—stories illustrated by nicely retouched photos and appropriate landscaping. Perhaps you yourself, in weak moments, have dreamed of finding such neglected old places, and of transforming them with much gay banter and a few hasty hammer strokes into charming little picture cottages.

If you are the hardy, take-things-in-your-stride type who can laugh off frozen glasses of water in your bedroom while you are putting in a heating system; if you can live perhaps for years in a state of continuous upset, with unfinished walls about you, lumber stacked in the yard, an apology for a kitchen, and the living room a shambles; if you can quote Thoreau as you lug pails of water up from the spring, all that we can say is that you are one of those born house-remodelers, and nothing will stop you. And no doubt you will come up with a book of your own about your house-remodeling adventures, and you will sell enough copies so that you won't have to live in the darn place!

Again, however, we are talking in this book to ordinary people—those who don't get too much fun out of living in an unfinished or inadequate house; who can't change their abodes every time their fancies dictate; who have to scrape or beg a minimum of money to make a cash down payment on their houses—and who have to borrow the rest. And we are talking to people who want a productive country home, a place where they can raise much of their own food—fruit, vegetables, eggs, and perhaps milk and meat. You can accomplish in spare time the task of setting up a producing homestead while you are rebuilding a little gray home off the road into a livable house—but it won't be easy. If you have the money and the time and the ability and the urge for such activity, then we wish you good luck.

However, let us not look with too jaundiced an eye on grandpa's house. He built according to his likes and the conveniences available at the time. Probably your descendants will laugh at your "modern" house—and there will be plenty to laugh at. In many cases grandpa built well, for his houses are still standing, while many professional so-called buildings, bungalows and half-timbered houses, built twenty years ago, are ready for the wrecker.

The country house—even of ancient vintage—is more likely to be a better candidate for remodeling than an old city or suburban house. The country house, after all, was built for country living, and aside from our modern heating, plumbing and lighting, the requirements of comfort haven't changed much. Sun, light, air and room continue to be just as essential.

Curiously enough, the older a house, the more it will lend itself to remodeling. Those of us who have seen the old houses of Newburyport, Salem, Williamsburg and Charleston, can testify to their grace and beauty. Such houses can be made entirely adequate for modern use with a surprisingly small amount of remodeling. But it is almost impossible for a family of moderate means to buy one of these houses at anything approaching a moderate price. He who is fortunate enough to find such a fine old house in the country has indeed unearthed a jewel.

THE VICTORIAN ERA

What you are more likely to be offered in your search is a house of the Victorian era, built between 1875 and 1914. Most of the houses erected in the elegant eighties, the gay nineties, and the lush 1900's reveal the bad taste of Victorian times. This was the era of large, sprawling, ornate structures, extravagant in ornament and material, and in efforts to imitate French chateaux, and English castles, and Greek temples.

This, too, was the era of large families, and so you will find houses with rooms cut up into cubbyholes to harbor the numerous offspring. And you will find *wood trim!* Victorian houses were jammed with it! Whenever grandpa saw an empty space, he put in some of that new-fangled scroll-work—that marvelous imitation of hand-carving! But you will find very few closets. Grandpa had wardrobes and chests and quantities of other portable storage space. And as we go through grandpa's kitchen and bathroom—well, let's just close our eyes!

You can remodel those houses, however, as they did have one big advantage. As a rule they were built very spaciously. And when you knock down their unsightly towers and battlements, their porticoes, porches, porte-cocheres, gables, and prisonlike windows, you may find that you have a pretty comfortable old place.

If you plan to live the Garden Way you will need adequate food processing space. Grandpa rated the inner man higher than some of his descendants, so you will undoubtedly find a good-sized kitchen in his house.

And even though the kitchen may not be large enough to install the modern processing and freezing equipment you may want, there is usually enough room in such old houses to tear down a partition and make a real "harvest room." In like manner the expanded storage requirements of the modern productive homestead can be taken care of readily through use of that spaciousness which grandpa invariably built into his house.

The Garden Way homestead needs plenty of storage space for garden tools and equipment, as well as shelter for any poultry or other livestock you may decide to raise. Grandpa's house usually had one or more outbuildings—a barn, or as it later became known, a "carriage house." There was a woodshed, and perhaps some other outbuildings original uses for which may now be forgotten. When the property contains such outbuildings, you can consider that, for the present at least, most of your barn and storage problems will be solved.

GARDENS

As to gardens, you will find that most old country houses do have some sort of garden. And, as often as not, you will find fruit trees in some state of production. They are likely, too, to have fully grown shrubs which former owners had added over the years. It takes a long time, you know, to grow luxuriant lilac bushes, wisteria vines and hydrangeas.

Another advantage of the old house is that it will undoubtedly have some landscaping. It may be that the trees and shrubs are not placed exactly as you would

This kind of alteration is usually economical. It consists mainly of eliminating undesirable features and often, at minor expense, adds greatly to the value of the house. Notice how the removal of Victorian gingerbread and the simple change in the porch and the entrance give an entirely new and more pleasing appearance. Grading of the lawn has covered up the unsightly views of the foundation.

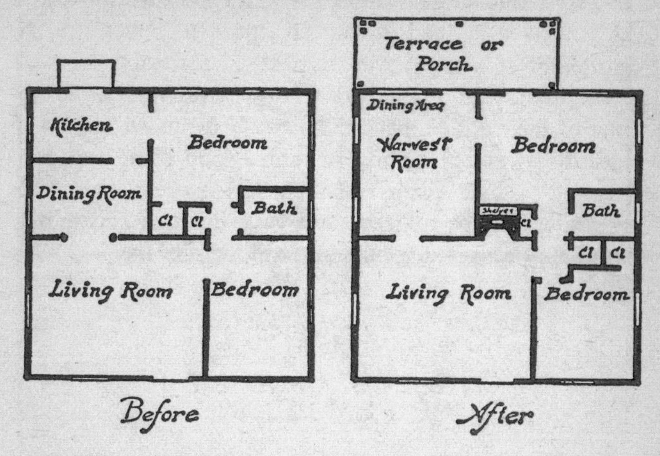

This is an inexpensive interior alteration which, by removal of a partition, gives a good-sized "harvest-room" instead of the cramped separate kitchen and dining room. Closet space has been added simply to a bedroom which lacked it and the living room has been made much more pleasant by the substitution of a fireplace for one of the closets in the master bedroom. At the same time, shelves have been retained in the bedroom as compensation for loss of part of the closet space.

like, but they may be very attractive and provide much needed shade in the summer. And you can't grow 40-foot trees in five years, either! If you want to make landscaping changes, you can do so gradually.

TOOLS AND UTILITIES

In buying country houses you may be fortunate, too, in finding a good supply of tools and equipment "thrown in" with the house. These are a most valuable asset, as you have learned if you have tried to buy tools or gardening equipment over the past several years.

Invariably, too, the older house will have at least one of the utilities that are so costly to install today—electricity, a septic tank, plumbing, and some type of heating system. Again, although they may not be modern, they can be utilized until your finances and more normal prices make it possible to modernize them.

THE ECONOMIC SIDE OF REMODELING

In most cases the question comes down to the economics of remodeling an old house as against building a new one. And here even the experts—the architects and the builders—will often be found in disagreement. But there are certain basic standards by which you may judge the comparative costs involved.

We wouldn't ask you to go into this study of basic standards if we didn't feel it necessary. But in your search for country property you are going to run into at least a dozen or more old houses which will be offered to you. Builders and architects consider it work, not pleasure, to accompany you on these scouting trips. You can't take one of them along to look at *every* house you are considering for their advice as to the practicability of remodeling. They will be willing to estimate the comparative cost of building or remodeling once you have more or less decided on a certain piece of property.

Speaking of architects, it's our firm opinion that their services are just as indispensable in remodeling as in new building. It takes the professional eye of an architect to visualize the *possibilities* of an existing structure, and his technical knowledge to *translate* those possibilities into practical and economical *realities.* Even though you plan to do the remodeling yourself, the counsel of an architect will more than pay for itself in the long run. By using the information in this chapter, you can eliminate some old houses as entirely unsuitable, and bring to the attention of the architect and builder only those that offer real potentialities for practical and desirable remodeling.

WHEN TO REMODEL

This brings us to the most important fundamental of remodeling. Usually remodeling is an economical operation *only* when it involves the removing of undesirable features—porches, turrets, nonbearing partitions, windows, etc. It becomes an *expensive operation* when remodeling necessitates adding any feature, such as plumbing, heating, a new lighting system, a new foundation, a new roof line or roof, adding a cellar or a story or a wing, or rebuilding a chimney. You must remember that it costs the same or more to add *new* construction or equipment to an *old* house as it does to build or add them to a *new* house.

Of course there are things that you can do to improve and modernize an old house that involve less expense, such as painting the exterior, removing porches or additions, taking down a few interior, nonbearing walls, adding windows and doors, installing new floors, or replacing trim.

MAJOR REPLACEMENTS AND REPAIRS

As a guide in arriving at the approximate costs involved in remodeling a house, we give below a list of items that most frequently require replacement or major repair. It is advisable to find out the average cost of these items and installations in your locality, and to fill in the figures in the table. If you are seriously considering a piece of property, take all necessary measure-

Table 4

Roofing	(Get current cost of gravel, asphalt or other roofing per 100 square feet.)
Flashing, gutters, downspouts	(Get current cost per lineal foot.)
Chimney flues or entire construction	(Get current cost per lineal foot.)
Concrete work	(Get current cost per cubic yard.)
Exterior stucco work	(Get current cost per square yard.)
Exterior painting	(Get current cost per square yard.)
Interior wooden walls	(Get current cost per lineal foot.)
New stairways	(Get current cost per step.)
Floor surfacing	(Get current cost per square foot.)
Interior plastering	(Get current cost per square yard.)
Plumbing	(Get current labor price per fixture, plus current cost of
Toilet, Lavatory, Bathtub, Shower, Kitchen	(Get current cost of sinks, counters, etc.)

ments. This will enable you to approach actual costs more closely, and will help you to determine whether you wish to call in expert counsel to confirm the advisability of buying.

The table of costs (above) for specific jobs is one

means of arriving at an approximation of remodeling costs. There is another and perhaps more comprehensive way of going about it. It is based on rule-of-thumb estimates which architects and builders customarily use for new-house construction, plus the proportion to the total cost of construction borne by the various elements of a building job.

This sounds more complicated than it is. Let us go at it step by step. Architects and builders estimate construction costs from either the total square feet or cubic feet of the house. If you are looking at an old house, it is not too difficult to figure roughly its size in square or cubic feet, as the dimensions will probably be available to you. You will figure attic space as half that of the floor below, and open porches at half the corresponding house space. Then get cost figures from several builders in the area to estimate the approximate original cost of the old house you are looking at.

To get down to hypothetical figures, let us assume you figure that a house of the type you are looking at, old and in poor condition, would cost $20,000 to build new. If, after deducting the appraised value of the land from the price of the property offered you, the indicated price of the above house is $12,000, you have the difference between that and $20,000, or $8,000 as the amount you can economically spend for remodeling.

Besides this useful bit of information, you now have another way of estimating remodeling costs. It has been figured that on the average the major elements of house construction bear these percentage relationships to the entire costs:

Roof: 7%	This means a totally new roof, covering all items from the frame outward. You can buy roofing materials of every vari-

ety, and at varying prices, so that it is important to decide on the type of roof you want. Don't forget the figure is an average one.

Walls: 16% — This would cover situations in which walls may have to be done over entirely, outside as well as inside. If expensive interior wall coverings are needed the cost might reach 18 to 20%. But walls can be repaired by reinforcing, stuccoing, shingling, etc.

Floors: 12% — This applies if the floors have to be entirely done over. Most floors need only surfacing, replacing of floor boards, varnishing, etc.

Electrical works: 5% — This is applicable where the entire electrical work has to be replaced. Usually, though, new outlets and new fixtures only have to be added.

Heating systems: — Percentages vary with the type of heating: For entirely new systems the average would be:

Hot Air	6%
Hot Water	10%
Electric	5%

Preferably heating systems should be new, except where there are good hot air ventilators, good hot water pipes or radiators which are usable. Sometimes a new furnace must be added. Or radiators only may have to be replaced. If you plan to use electric heating there may be a large additional expense in improving the insulation of the house or your electric bills will be enormous.

Plumbing: 5% — This is the estimated percentage based on a need for entirely new plumbing, from cellar to roof. What is more likely to be needed are some of the items given in the table on page 116.

Let us suppose your hypothetical candidate for remodeling seems to need entire replacement only of the roof, walls and plumbing. The percentages add up to 28, and this applied to $20,000 is $5,600. Subtracting this from $8,000, you find yourself with $2,400 left to pay for the minor repairs and replacements.

Your inexperienced estimate of what is needed to be done is likely to be too low. When an architect or builder answers your call he will probably find any number of things wrong that you did not suspect. So be prepared for a higher figure than the one you reach yourself.

BUILDING YOUR OWN HOME

We have outlined most of the advantages, as well as the disadvantages of buying the older type of country house. Let us now briefly consider the advantages of building your own home. To begin with, it can be built in accordance with the specific needs of yourself and your family. You may have the benefit of every modern advance in home building—architecturally, structurally and functionally. The new house can offer more of those conveniences which we associate with modern living. It can be erected quickly, and is ready for immediate, comfortable living. It can be built on land of your own choosing, and so oriented on the land as to take advantage of our modern ideas of the use of sun, light, air and outlook. While offering sufficient space for living, it is adaptable for expansion, and it need not be extravagant of space. It is bright, new and more easily maintained than an older house. It can—it should be—especially designed for our productive concept of country living—for the Garden Way. The cost of erecting a new house can be figured in advance, within reasonable limits. Provision can be made for future expansion, but essentially the newly-built house is a "package" of known utility and cost.

SHOULD YOU REMODEL?

This brings up the conflict which often arises as to the relative advantages or disadvantages of building a new house as against remodeling an old one. This is likely to be decided on the basis of sentiment. You come across an old house which your wife insists was "just made for us," and presto!—you are planning to put the place into shape. Or you yourself are going to take a fancy to the lines of some forgotten farm house, overgrown with vines, nestling under an ancient tree. In your mind's eye—with no little help from the real estate man—you see the old place restored, the sagging doorstep raised, the front yard cleared and planted with hollyhocks, the holes in the roof repaired.

It is quite likely, however, that you will find that the old place has nothing but its lines to recommend it. The converted coal furnace gives heat downstairs; there is none in the upstairs bedrooms; its floors sag and the beams in the cellar are slowly giving way. It has no insulation, no ventilation and all the sills are rotted.

Many a family has bought such a wreck almost solely because of its charming, sagging lines. Yet the lines are only the exterior walls; they represent only 16 per cent of the total value. So even if such a house were quoted at $10,000 you would still be getting only $1600 worth of wall—which in all probability would be worthless anyway for keeping out winter blasts.

All this may sound discouraging to the family which is yearning to "do over" an old house. If you stopped to consider the amount of money you would have to pour into such a house, you would find that it wouldn't be a very profitable or satisfactory undertaking, even if you got the house for *nothing.* If you *must* have that particular location, it would be far better to tear down the relic and put up a new house with the enchanting lines you found in the old one.

WHEN IT PAYS TO REMODEL

On the other hand, an old house—if livable—*has* advantages from a financial point of view. Under ordinary circumstances all the financial "water" has been squeezed out of it. If the original owner had paid too much for it, he and perhaps subsequent owners have paid for their mistakes, and it has probably reached its normal level by now. Many old houses have important features—greenhouses, landscaping, roadways, fences—which would cost plenty today. And in most cases their locations have been time-tested. They have had a chance to "take root" in the soil. Under average circumstances, too, there is a greater leeway in bargaining for an older house than in building a new one. There may be urgent reasons for selling, so that irrespective of the value, the price may be low. And if the price is low enough, there is a distinct saving of money—especially to the family willing and able to do much of its own remodeling and repairing. Often the owner will sell for a fairly low cash down payment, and take a mortgage for the rest. But even though the owner doesn't want a

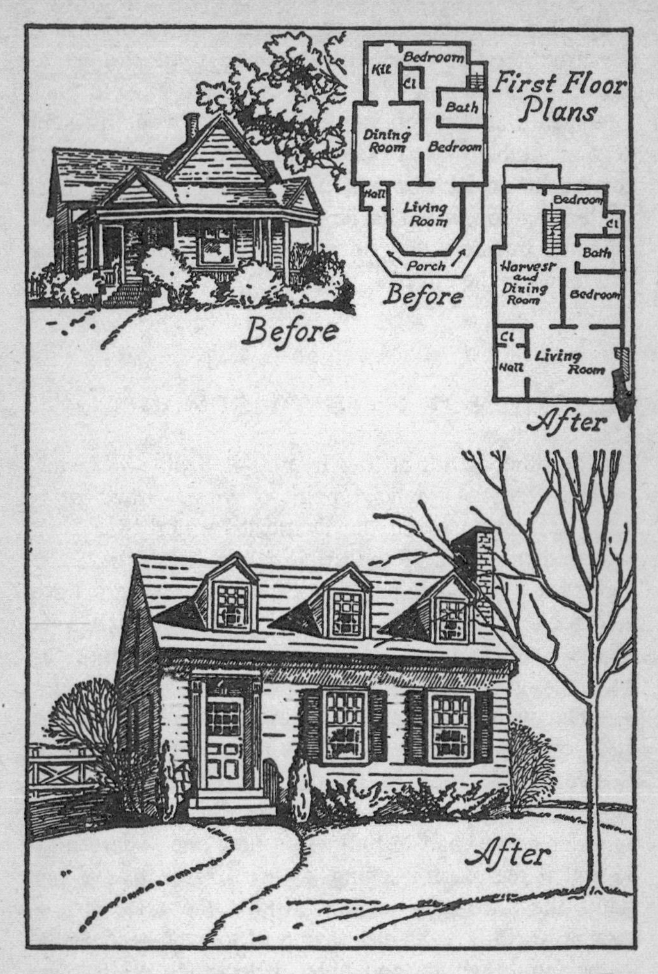

This is the type of alteration which is so extensive that it frequently costs almost as much as building a whole new house. Note that in addition to removing the old-fashioned porch, the roof has been entirely changed. The plans used also reveal very drastic changes in the ground floor arrangement.

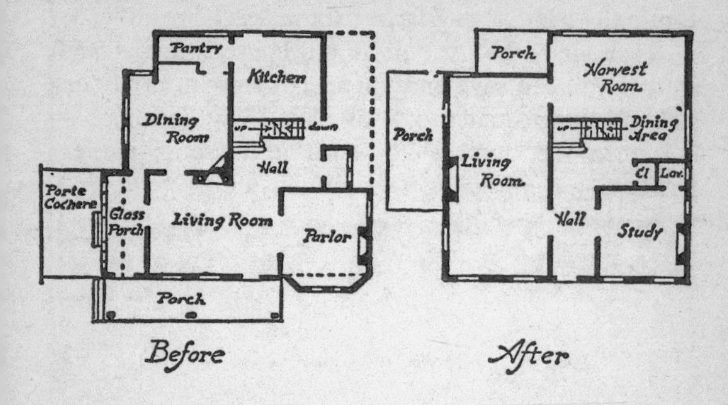

This alteration, in addition to eliminating some of the interior partitions, involves a drastic rearrangement of the floor space and new walls on all four sides. It is doubtful whether changes of this type could be justified economically.

mortgage, the price may be low enough so you can get your mortgage from the bank. If you need little or no bank financing, interest and financing charges are cut down, and the house becomes yours sooner. A low cash price and a small mortgage will relieve you of a long-term burden of debt.

If the old house is livable, repairs can be made gradually. New or second-hand material can be bought for cash. Labor costs usually represent at least 50 per cent of the cost of any operation, so that if you are able to do most of the work yourself, you can always remain in a better cash position than would be the case if you had to pay a larger amount for a new house. This is an important consideration, even if you are forced to go through a period of almost continuous upset while the remodeling is going on. To many families freedom from constantly overhanging large debt makes it worth while.

All in all, if the price of an old house is low enough so that you can save an appreciable amount even considering the estimated cost of remodeling and improving, then the purchase of such a house is entirely justified.

Chapter Seven

HOW TO GET THE MOST MORTGAGE FOR THE LEAST MONEY

For the majority of people financing represents the very crux of their property-buying transactions. Country living can be a serene and rewarding way of life *if* your country property is financed properly. More failures to achieve the goal of happy country living are attributable to ill considered and unsuitable financing than to any other cause. The reasons for this are simple. Land and home ownership are so interwoven with sentiment, with the dreams and desires of the rent-paying family, that the stubborn facts of financing often are ignored or hastily brushed aside.

We trust, therefore, that this chapter will be helpful to those who have given little or no thought to the problems of financing; that it will caution those who might otherwise be tempted to make hasty financial decisions, and that it will encourage those who set their sights sensibly on horizons which are not too remote to attain.

Reduced to its simplest fundamentals, there are two ways of financing country property. It can be bought either for cash, or for part cash and part borrowed money—or what is known as a mortgage.

Practically every expert on property matters agrees that the wisest policy is to pay as much cash on your property as you can safely spare—all cash if possible. The reason is simply that money is a costly commodity, especially in these times of high interest rates. If you are one of those fortunate few able to pay full cash for your property, the counsel given here may not assume quite so much importance for you. Yet we feel that you, too, can profit by reading it, if it helps answer some of the many specious arguments that have been thought up to influence people against paying cash for property.

THE NEXT BEST SOLUTION

The second best solution to paying all cash for your property is to buy on a real pay-as-you-go basis. This presupposes starting by buying your land for cash and building the smallest possible living units; paying cash for these units, and then gradually adding other units as fast as you acquire the further cash to do so.

The third situation, the one in which the majority of country property buyers find themselves, involves the purchase of a house and acreage necessitating financing by means of a mortgage. This transaction will require a down payment varying in amount in accordance with individual circumstances, and securing a mortgage for the balance.

A *mortgage* is a written promise to pay back a debt, with the property—*and usually more*—as security. Most mortgages provide that the money be paid back either in whole or in part by a given date. If payment is not made in accordance with the terms of the mortgage, the person who executes the mortgage loses his right or "title" to the property, and ownership passes to the lending institution which made the loan. The legal action to regain the property is called an action of *foreclosure and sale* in most states.

The amount of money you borrow on a mortgage is called the principal. Money is a commodity, and must be paid for like everything else. The method of figuring the amount you must pay is through what is known as the *rate of interest.* This represents a certain percentage of the total loan or principal. Interest is computed on the unpaid balance and is usually paid with a portion of the principal as part of equal monthly installments. This is called an amortizing mortgage, the type that was developed in the 1940's, primarily to suit the needs of the majority of people who are employed on a fixed salary, and paid at regular weekly, bi-monthly and monthly intervals. It is defined as a mortgage in which the principal is reduced and eventually paid up completely by regular monthly, quarterly, semi-annual or annual payments, at the same time that regular interest payments are made on the unpaid balance.

The mortgages which provide for quarterly, or less frequent, payments are advantageous to the lender, as interest payments are slightly higher, and his bookkeeping entries are minimized. But such payments are none too desirable for the family which receives its income in the form of weekly, bi-monthly or monthly salaries. Sums must be accumulated and set aside to meet the due-date. Some methodical families can do that without any trouble, but there is a great temptation to spend the money otherwise.

The monthly payment plan is the most advantageous for the average property buyer. (It is also a protection to the lender.) One of the principal advantages of the monthly payment plan is that it promptly brings to the attention of both the borrower and the lender any change in the financial picture of the borrower. As soon as you fail to make a payment on time you begin to hear from the lending institution. This attention may seem inconsiderate, but the system has its merits. On the one hand the borrower is made to pay up promptly, if he possibly can, and that is to his benefit. If misfortune is back of his failure to maintain his payments, and his record is good, extensions are often granted. By contrast, with the old yearly-payment straight mortgage, the situation frequently got out of hand before any need was seen for remedial measures.

FIXED MONTHLY PAYMENT PLAN

The usual fixed monthly payment plan for the amortized mortgage provides for equal monthly payments throughout the full duration of the instrument. For example, suppose you borrowed $1,000 for a ten-year period at the interest rate of 4 per cent. This would obligate you to make 120 monthly payments during that period.

These payments would amount to $10.31 a month, including amortization and interest.

At the beginning, because you would be paying interest on almost the total amount of the mortgage, most of the $10.31 would be needed to cover the interest. The small balance would represent payment applied toward amortization of the principal. However, as you continued to make payments, the interest would be figured on decreasing amounts of unpaid principal. Therefore the proportion represented by interest would then decrease, while the proportion applied toward amortization of the principal would increase.

Below is a table giving the monthly payments due on mortgages of $1,000 at 6, 7, and 8 per cent interest. Tables such as the one below have been worked out for every mortgage amount, rate of interest and period, and your lending institution should be able to supply such tables to you on request.

$1,000 Amortized in 10 years

At each month you would pay	6% $11.10	7% $11.61	8% $12.13
At the end of the:	You would owe	You would owe	You would owe
First year	1,198.80	1,253.88	1,310.00
Second year	1,065.60	1,114.56	1,164.48
Third year	932.40	975.24	1,018.92
Fourth year	799.20	835.92	873.36
Fifth year	666.00	696.60	727.80
Sixth year	532.80	557.28	582.24
Seventh year	399.60	417.96	436.68
Eighth year	266.40	278.64	291.12
Ninth year	133.20	139.32	145.56
Tenth year	Paid	Paid	Paid

The monthly amounts due for a mortgage of $5,000, $10,000, $15,000 or $20,000 would be approximately, five, ten, fifteen, and twenty times the above amounts.

TAXES AND INSURANCE

Lending institutions have a good deal of interest in whether you, as a borrower on a mortgage, pay your real estate taxes. Default in tax payments could lead to loss of your property through a forced tax sale. The lender also wants to be sure that any buildings under the mortgage are fully covered by fire insurance, in which the lender is the first beneficiary in the event of a loss.

So in one way or another the lender seeks to make sure you are paying your taxes and keeping up your insurance. Sometimes these payments are made by the lender for you, and collected from you as part of the monthly payments.

MORTGAGE EXTENSION PERIODS

The question of the stationary mortgage interest rate often comes up for discussion in real estate circles. The interest is partly a compensation for the risk the lender takes with his money. But as his money is repaid to him, with interest, and he has less and less at stake in the property, his risk *decreases*. The borrower, if he has paid promptly, has proved that he is a good risk, yet he continues to pay the same rate of interest as if he were an unproved risk—or so the argument goes. It is not improbable that in mortgage plans of the future, provision will be made for a lessening interest rate as the borrower continues to pay.

NEW MORTGAGE PROVISIONS

Nothing is more changeable than the fortunes of the average family over a period of ten to twenty years. Hence, along with the greater flexibility of mortgage plans today have come provisions which to some extent adapt the mortgage to the changing financial picture of the borrower. He may be in a position to make larger amortization payments than the mortgage calls for—or to pay in full before the term of the mortgage has ended, thus saving interest payments.

Provision for stepped-up payments, or payment in full, is to the advantage of the borrower, and some institutions are reluctant to make this concession. Usually the mortgage lender will require a penalty of some type if the mortgage is prepaid before maturity. Especially is this the case with the current high interest rate levels at which it is to the lender's advantage to extend your repayment for as long as possible in order to reap maximum return in interest. In other words, as a condition of making a loan, incurring record-keeping costs, etc., lenders may require a penalty of 1 per cent or 2 per cent of the loan principal, if the loan is paid off within a shorter time than maturity, and therefore with less return to him than anticipated.

Another method is to permit 20 per cent of the remaining amount to be prepaid in any one year without penalty; if completely paid off, then 90 to 120 days interest must be paid by the borrower as a penalty but only as applicable to 80 per cent of the loan outstanding. These arrangements vary widely with lenders and with their relative bargaining position at the time, as well as with interest rates and money supply. At the moment, as in the case of other tight money situations, lenders are in a good bargaining position. Borrowers should be alert to avoid being "locked in" to a high interest rate because of the possibility of later refinancing the loan at a lower rate. This, however, is a matter to be understood and bargained for at the time of arranging the loan. Consider yourself either lucky or a good bargainer if today no prepayment penalty is required in your mortgage contract.

By far the more frequent problem, however, is that of meeting payments during periods of unemployment, illness or financial stress.

Opinion has grown to the effect that the buyer of property who has met his indebtedness promptly over a period of years has earned the privilege of a so-called "grace period" to tide him over a period of stringency. One provision gives the borrower a grace period of one month for each year of prompt payment following a minimum payment period of from three to six years. For example, if you had met your payments regularly for six years, and then found yourself in a tight spot financially, you would be entitled to a grace period on amortization of one month for each of these years, or a total of six months. Most likely you would be asked, though, to pay the interest, taxes, and insurance. Naturally it would be necessary for you to make up these suspended principal payments sometime before the end of the mortgage period.

Another type of mortgage allows you to defer payment on your principal if you make prepayment of amounts in excess of those you had originally agreed to pay. For example, if your original mortgage agreement stipulated that you were to pay off $200 a year on your principal, and you had, over a three-year period, made payments of $300 a year, you could defer principal payments until the amount due had caught up with the amount you had actually paid.

If it is impossible for you to secure a mortgage with the type of provisions outlined above (and such mortgages should be available), at least you should arrange for a mortgage which will safeguard you against immediate or premature foreclosure in the event of nonpayment of any installment. You can insist, certainly, on a grace period of from fifteen to thirty days—even more, as a minimum—before any such foreclosure action is taken, the grace period to increase in proportion to the amount of equity you have attained in the property. As a matter of fact some states require such a sliding grace period, the extent of the period being fixed by judges sitting in equity.

SPECIAL FEATURES

In some sections where competition to place mortgage loans is keen, you will find so-called loan "plans" or "systems" which seem to offer advantages other than those obtained in the standard type loans. Such features might be the inclusion (charged to you, of course) of the cost of home equipment. This would probably wear out long before the entire loan had been paid—yet the interest on the cost of such installations would be made a part of the entire loan. These "new features" or "special advantages" correspond in a way to the gadgets which car manufacturers add to their cars to influence a sale. They are usually insignificant in the long run, and are played up out of all proportion to their value to you.

Get the basic facts of your loan; analyze its monthly charges and its features in accordance with the principles given here, and don't give too much thought to "special features."

WHO LENDS MONEY—AND HOW MUCH

Mortgage loans aren't made by machinery. They are arranged *by* people, *for* people. That lender may be a bank, a building and loan association, an insurance company—at least part of whose function is the business of lending money. The lender is going to charge you as much as he thinks he can reasonably get. This is why the initial conferences between you and the lender may sometimes evolve into a battle of wits. It is all the more reason why you should know your lender; why you should apply care and common sense in choosing him; and why it is so important to know your *rights* as well as your responsibilities when borrowing money.

On the other hand, you must appreciate that most modern lenders, particularly established financial institutions, make no attempt to "overload" borrowers with mortgages, the provisions of which they know can't be carried out. Nor do they charge higher interest rates than the average in the locality.

The wise lender can be of much help to you. He wants you to be able to meet your mortgage obligations. He doesn't relish foreclosing on property on which he has loaned money. In the first place, foreclosure is not often a profitable transaction for the lending institution. In the second place, a bank or lending institution which acquires the reputation of quick or extensive foreclosure won't get the bulk of the lending business.

Just as you are entitled to buy goods from any seller you choose, in like manner you are entitled to make preliminary investigation of as many leading institutions as you choose. Make no commitments whatever in the matter of "buying" your mortgage until your investigation is completed. Tell the lender frankly that you are considering buying country property; that you want to check on the various loan plans available in your vicinity. Previously your only sources for getting a loan were through one or two local banks in the community. They were in the enviable position of being able to dictate any terms they chose. But with the advent of insurance companies and other lending organizations into the national field, there is now competition in the mortgage loan business, redounding to the benefit of the borrower.

Remember that your preliminary negotiations for a loan are in the nature of exploratory talks. There is no compulsion to disclose your full financial position although you may choose to do so. You may offer a rough idea of your financial resources only, if you prefer, but of course you can expect only tentative estimates of the amount you can borrow, information on mortgage plans available, and terms.

The principal value of such exploratory talks is the fact that they will enable you to determine whether the institution is friendly, sound, and cooperative; a good firm with which to do business. Your friends can help you here. If they have taken out mortgages with the institution, and are frank with you, they can throw much light on the character of the organization. You may get conflicting opinions and reactions, and your best judgment will have to dictate your final course of action, uninfluenced by their own personal attitudes.

That the lending institution should be experienced in country property financing goes without saying. There are few banks and trust companies that are not. Occasionally you will come across an old type of institution that caters to a wealthy clientele, large commercial firms, or "estates." Some lenders act only as brokers. Immediately upon granting a mortgage they sell it to some other bank or investment corporation. This results in an immediate loss of the personal relationship which you should have with your lending institution.

Some lending institutions are limited in the variety of mortgage plans they can offer. It would be more desirable to do business with an institution having a number of flexible plans for mortgage loans, such as have been developed over the past few years.

Remember that in arranging a mortgage loan you are entering upon a long-time association with the lending institution—perhaps twenty or thirty years. The personnel in banks and institutions changes. The pleasant chap you liked so much when you negotiated your loan may be replaced by someone who isn't as approachable. Try to be objective about the institution, rather than permit yourself to be influenced by one personality there. View the institution as a whole—the general atmosphere—the general type of the staff.

On the other hand, don't build up an adverse opinion of a lending institution just because they will not grant everything you ask for. Remember that they have a more objective view of your financial status than *you* have. They may actually be doing you a kindness in denying your request at a particular time. They may save your "biting off more than you can chew." Take their refusal in that spirit, and adjust your sights accordingly. You will never get into trouble by *under*-borrowing.

BANKS AS LENDERS

There are three kinds of banks—commercial banks, savings banks, and trust companies. If you are a business man, you have probably done business with commercial banks. They generally make short-term loans to business firms. They rarely consider mortgage loans. Commercial banks having savings departments often make mortgage loans through that department.

Savings banks do make mortgage loans, as you no doubt know. It is their practice to invest a certain proportion of the savings entrusted to them in mortgages. It is through these investments that they are enabled to pay interest on the accounts of their savings depositors.

Trust companies are organized, as the name implies, to handle the funds of corporations, estates and individuals, making sales, transfers, decisions, and other financial arrangements for them. Trust companies generally maintain mortgage departments, and make mortgage loans.

BANKS AND SAVINGS AND LOANS

Small town banks and savings and loans are good sources of conventional mortgage credit, and in some cases may be easier to deal with than metropolitan area banks. Local banks and savings and loans may lend up to 75 to 80 per cent of the value or purchase price for twenty to twenty-five years. If the latter have arrangements with private mortgage loan insurance firms which guarantee the upper portion of the loan, they may make up to 90 per cent mortgages. However, the bank and savings and loans' terms in these days of "tight money" may tend to be more restrictive than this in some areas. Under some state usury laws establishing maximum interest rates, lenders may be allowed to charge discount "points" which result in a higher yield; in other states this may be prohibited. Rapidly climbing interest rates in recent months have collided with long-established usury laws in some states virtually to shut-off mortgage funds.

Therefore, if you can persuade a property owner to take back a mortgage, possibly at a lower than current interest rate, you may save substantially. If this is not feasible and if local banks and savings and loans in surrounding towns are loaned to the hilt, or if you do not have 20-25 per cent or more in cash to make a down payment, there are other ways to approach your purchase.

FHA AND FHDA FINANCING

The Federal Housing Administration (FHA), a Federal government agency, has low down payment, insured loan programs suitable for new or existing homes in small towns as well as larger cities. Banks and real estate agents should know which lenders in a given locality are qualified and approved to arrange such loans.

An FHA-approved lender provides the money at a current maximum of 7½ per cent interest today, but may have to impose discount "points" to bring the yield to the going market rate. An FHA mortgage insurance premium of ½ per cent must be paid, making it at least an effective 8 per cent rate to the borrower.

FHA provides insurance to the lender against loss; this encourages the lender to make low down payment loans he might not otherwise be inclined to supply and for terms up to thirty years. FHA-insured mortgage down payments are substantially below conventional loans: 3 per cent on values up to $15,000, plus 10 per cent of value up to $20,000, plus 20 per cent of value up to $30,000. (Congress may ease these further in the future.)

Banks, mortgage bankers, or mortgage correspondents which have been designated as approved FHA lenders are usually the best sources for this kind of financing. There is a certain amount of red-tape connected with FHA mortgages not present for conventional, non-insured type loans, but the lender in the main handles this. This is important to understand—

private lenders make the money available, not the FHA.

FHA loans are most feasible in cities and towns of more than 5,500 population. Farmers Home Administration (FHDA) loans are most feasible in towns below that figure and in rural or outlying areas. It is often erroneously assumed that Farmers Home (FHDA) loans are made only to actual farmers; in fact, some 80 per cent of such transactions benefit rural families not earning their living on farms. FHDA-insured home loans are made available through some 1,600 local county Farmers Home supervisors (instead of private lenders, as with FHA) for families on farms or in "rural non-farm areas" who are unable to obtain credit on comparable terms. Low and moderate income families may qualify for special interest saving benefits.

Such loans may be for purchase or construction of single family dwellings or for a dwelling in open country or village—not part of an urban area. Mortgages are made for up to thirty-three years, at an interest rate of 7½ per cent for those families above moderate incomes, 6¼ per cent for those of low to moderate incomes and less than that for those of very low income. Due to great demand for such loans, the FHDA is not always in a position to accommodate all applicants; however, where location criteria apply, inquiries as to availability of such financing may be wise.

If you are a veteran, another source of financing assistance is through the GI Loan Bill. Information can be received through the local lending institutions, or an office of the Veterans Administration.

CONSTRUCTION LOANS

If a family decides to select land and have a house built by contracting with a local builder, but requires financing, an interim construction loan is usually arranged from which the builder is allowed to draw advances at specified intervals of construction progress. The bank or savings and loan will have to approve the contract, will want a survey, title insurance, etc.

Upon completion, a permanent mortgage is signed and recorded; at that time the construction loan is paid off, and the builder receives his final payment from the mortgage proceeds. The owner moves in. In some cases if the construction lender and permanent lender are the same institution, the transaction becomes in effect one loan at the same rate. If two lenders are involved, separate transactions occur. The pattern is practically the same where FHA is involved except for certain red-tape, primarily of concern to the lender.

REMODELING

Financing remodeling can be handled in a number of ways: (1) obtaining a personal bank loan; an FHA Title I remodeling loan; a bank or savings and loan (non-FHA) remodeling loan; (2) refinancing an existing mortgage (but watch out for today's higher interest rates); (3) in the case of an older house, securing a commitment from the lender to include prescribed remodeling costs in the purchase mortgage on the basis of the increased value of the remodeled house; (4) negotiating a second mortgage, which usually involves a higher interest rate than the first mortgage but for a shorter term; (5) obtaining FHDA loans, when available, in rural areas. You may want to do your own remodeling; but depending on the type of financing arranged for, the lender may need assurance that you are competent to execute it.

SATISFACTION OF MORTGAGE

When you make your final payment on a mortgage, you will receive the original mortgage that you signed. Accompanying it will be a certificate testifying to the fact that the mortgage has been paid or "satisfied." This is called a "satisfaction piece" or "satisfaction of the mortgage," and must be either filed or recorded, whichever your local statute may require. It is your responsibility to see that such satisfaction is either filed or recorded, in compliance with the law, or to see that the lending institution does it. The absence of a record of "satisfaction of the mortgage" has been the basis of many a law suit!

Ten or twenty years is a long time. Records of payment are lost or mislaid; checks and stubs disappear; bank records may be impossible to get. There is the possibility of a situation developing which you might be unable to offer *real* proof of the fact that you paid your mortgage. Perhaps this will impress on you the *absolute importance* of properly recording and filing your "satisfaction of the mortgage." Incidentally it wouldn't be a bad idea to keep your own check-stubs or cancelled checks or receipts of mortgage payments in a safety deposit box. You can never tell when the question of your payment or non-payment might come up.

Chapter Eight

CHECK THESE TWENTY-FIVE SOURCES OF TROUBLE BEFORE BUYING

Up to the point of committing yourself definitely to the purchase of a piece of country property, you are free to change your mind as often as you wish, make additional requests of property owners, and shop around freely for a mortgage offering the best possible terms.

However, once you have decided on a particular piece of property, other people enter the picture immediately. As many as a dozen persons may be involved in the transfer of a particular piece of property, aside from the friends you may call in for counsel and advice. We are bringing this to your attention, not out of a desire to make the transaction appear complicated, but to impress on you the extreme importance of taking certain steps, legal and otherwise, to safeguard yourself against what might afterwards develop into possible sources of annoyance and expense.

Subsequent to your decision to buy a specific piece of property, there are three steps that it becomes imperative for you to take for full protection of your interests. They are:

(1) Get as many agreements, reports, understandings, promises—anything which either you or the others involved plan or intend to do, *in writing*. Memories are short, and what is entirely clear to you and everyone else today disappears into uncertainty tomorrow. There follows the familiar barrage of; "But you said," "It was my understanding," "I thought you meant," "You distinctly agreed," etc. You can't, of course, expect that every statement made by every person to whom you talk about the transaction be put in writing. Common sense will show the way. If you can't get a formal written agreement on certain points that you consider important, ask the person concerned to state what he is willing to do in a letter. If this suggestion meets with too much hesitation or resistance, the same result can be obtained by *your* writing the letter, outlining fully your understanding of the terms of the agreement, and asking that it be confirmed by letter. Enclosing a stamped, self-addressed envelope will almost invariably bring a note of confirmation. Your letter plus the confirmation of the person involved represents a far stronger support of any claim

you might make in the future than would be the verbal recollections of both of you, alone.

(2) Get receipts for all money which you pay out if at all possible. Get receipts even if you pay by check. Or, when you pay by check, accompany it with a letter stating that you are enclosing payment, and give the details as to what the payment covers. It would be a good idea to add on your letter the statement: "If this is not correct, please let me know at once." Nonreply generally implies agreement. We recommend this because while a cancelled check is indicative of *payment*, it offers no evidence of payment of a *specific thing*. Such receipts can also be requested "for your records." However, if the amount involved is too small to warrant going to so much trouble, and there is resistance, the matter can be handled simply and gracefully by writing the purpose of the payment on the back of the check, below the usual space for endorsement. Acceptance and endorsement of the check is then tantamount to an O.K. of the purpose.

(3) Before you sign any papers pertaining to your property transaction, read them very carefully. Be sure you understand *clearly* everything you are asked to sign. Most papers connected with property-buying are couched in legal or semi-legal phraseology. A single word in the document which may not be clear to you might carry a great deal of legal import. This may be just as true of the omission of a single significant word.

With these three general precautions in mind, we will now proceed to a discussion of the twenty-five important steps to be aware of in buying your country property. Some people attempt to go through this legal procedure without the counsel of a lawyer. We consider this most unwise, comparable to attempting to treat yourself for a serious ailment without consulting a doctor. Often a real estate broker will dismiss these subsequent legal technicalities casually, assuring you that he will take care of everything. But remember, he gets his commission from the seller, and even with the best intentions in the world he can't serve two masters.

Without question, you need a lawyer to see you through these legal steps. And don't expect him to do all your thinking for you. He can't possibly be as familiar with what you want as you are. But he can protect your rights and explain the meaning of the legal phraseology involved, so that you will know what you are signing. Spending the few dollars entailed in engaging the services of a lawyer may save you literally thousands of dollars in costly errors, not to mention heartache.

We are ready, now, to take up one by one the twenty-five steps you will have to take, going into an explanation of their meaning, and the method by which you can eliminate present or future trouble regarding each step.

(1 and 2) The Binder and Deposit

When you finally decide on a particular piece of country property, when you are satisfied with the price and terms, and have a reasonable expectation of being able to finance the purchase, your first step will be to sign an offer to buy the property. Your second step will be to pay a deposit on it as evidence of good faith, and to induce the seller to hold the property for you. This offer to buy is called a binder, and the money paid is, of course, a deposit. The amount of such a deposit may be anywhere from $100 to $1000—rarely more on a transaction under $20,000. In a few states even though you have signed a binder or offer to buy, and have paid a deposit, you still have the privilege of withdrawing the offer before the owner of the property accepts it in writing. The seller, however, has a similar privilege; he may reject your deposit and binder if he finds anything to his disadvantage within the corresponding time. In either case your money would be refunded. But, by and large, unless you can show gross misrepresentation on the seller's part, once an offer is made and a deposit paid, you cannot change your mind without losing your deposit.

There is, however, a less binding procedure which you may use prior to the binder and deposit, if you prefer, which is called an option. Under an option the owner of a piece of property gives you a written agreement to sell you the property at a specified price within a limited, specified number of days from the signing of the option, and you agree to notify the owner within that time of your intention. Generally you are required to pay a small sum, usually $50 to $100, which is not returnable, for the privilege of this service, and to recompense the owner for this lapse of time and for binding him to a price. If you are pretty much convinced that you want a certain property, but feel that you require a little additional time to clear up some question you might have about it, taking an option is a very desirable step.

You understand, of course, that the deposit you place on the property when you sign the binder is subsequently credited to the down payment which you make. The deposit should be held by the real estate broker in an escrow account until consummation of the sale.

(3) The Sales Contract

When the seller accepts both the binder and your deposit, your next step will be to sign a formal sales contract, sometimes called a purchase contract. This sales contract involves making a down payment on property consisting of a house and land, and involves, also, the matter of arranging for a mortgage. As we have already mentioned, when land alone is bought, full cash payment for it is generally required. The sales contract is always prepared in writing, and includes, insofar as is possible, all the terms of the sale. Remember, however, that once you sign the sales contract, you no longer have any bargaining power. You can't claim or ask for anything that isn't stipulated or listed in the sales contract. The sales contract becomes a most important instrument, then, and it would be well for you to give careful consideration to the subsequent steps discussed under Nos. 4 to 15 so as to assure yourself of the fact that everything of consequence is covered in your sales contract. Be sure that the seller's wife signs this contract as well as the deed, as legal difficulties could arise from her "dower" rights to the property.

(4) The Survey

A survey is a plan of the property, showing its exact dimensions, its boundaries, its varying levels, and a summary of every physical aspect of the property it is possible to obtain. You should get your architect, a builder, or a real estate lawyer to describe to you how a survey is made, and you should learn to read a survey reasonably well. It is not a difficult thing to do. The buyer usually pays for the survey. A survey should be made and included as part of the sales contract if at all possible, as it is the legal record of the exact size, area, and location of the property. A survey is usually asked for by banks and lending institutions, if you apply to them for a mortgage loan. Most of the larger acreages have never been surveyed in country districts—merely bounded by the names of adjacent owners. Country banks will sometimes accept such boundaries. A survey is an excellent thing to have, first, because it will help you in planning the subsequent use of your land, and, secondly, it will serve as evidence in case of a dispute over land, boundaries, water rights, etc. It should be recorded with the deed in the local land records.

(5) Date of Possession

Your purchase contract should stipulate the exact date on which the seller agrees to deliver the property. When buying land alone this is not so important, as ownership of the land takes place immediately following purchase.

However, in some country properties you will find that tenants rather than the owner occupy the premises. There is a possibility that the tenants have a lease with the present owner, which may run beyond the date on which you plan to take possession. There have been many cases where squatters have taken possession of country houses or outbuildings, where law suits were necessary to oust them. You should make the seller responsible either for providing you with legal possession on the date specified, or have him agree to indemnify you—that is, reimburse you for any expenses you may be forced to incur as a result of your inability to occupy the premises on the specified date.

(6) Pro-rating of Taxes

You should make the seller responsible for the payment of all taxes, assessments, and other obligations, up to the date of your taking possession. If you seek a mortgage, the lending institution will insist upon such payment anyway, before it grants you a mortgage. The seller should declare in the sales contract that all obligations have been paid—otherwise you might be held responsible for unpaid bills on the property. If the seller has paid taxes for the full year, and you take possession prior to the expiration of that period, the seller is entitled to a pro-rata reimbursement of the excess taxes he has paid.

(7) Pending Insurance

If the property you are buying is covered by insurance for the period between your purchase contract and your taking possession of the property, be sure that protection for you is written into the purchase contract. The risk of loss resulting from fire, hurricane, flood, or accident is yours, the buyer's, from the date you sign the purchase contract until the date you take possession. If the building were destroyed by fire during that period, for example, and there was no insurance coverage on the property, you would be held liable for the full purchase price of the property! If there is no insurance on the property at the time of the sales contract take it out at that time! Make sure that any existing insurance coverage is adequate.

(8) Description of Property

In addition to the survey which should be made a part of your purchase contract, be sure that the contract contains in writing the exact description of the house and land as described in the survey. Your lawyer should check this for you. Most arguments arise over the amount of acreage included in your purchase. In a controversy over this point, the court will recognize your legal right only to the number of acres specified in your purchase contract. If your purchase is made on a price per acre basis and you are in doubt about the precise number of acres you should most certainly have a survey made, so that the total number of acres may be written into the purchase contract. If you do not have a survey, be sure the contract stipulates that the sales price includes *all* the land owned by the seller in this piece of property, described by boundaries, with so many acres "plus or minus."

(9) Fixtures with Property

When you buy a piece of land, you are entitled to everything firmly attached to the land. When a house is included with the land, you are entitled to everything firmly attached to the house. But in buying country property it is often a moot question as to what is considered firmly attached to the land or house. There are certain things which we all recognize as integral parts of a piece of property, such as artesian wells, water and other pumps, lighting plants, windmills, tractors, loose lumber, gates, wire—even standing crops. These should be specified, and if the seller has agreed to include anything else, whether firmly fixed or not, as an inducement to get you to buy, these should be itemized in the purchase contract. Don't lose sight of the fact at any time that you cannot demand or make a claim for anything not specifically itemized in the purchase contract, and not clearly part of the property.

(10) Date of Deed Delivery

The date on which the seller agrees to deliver the deed should be stated specifically in the purchase contract. Sometimes the title to a piece of property isn't clear, but the question may not arise until an attempt is made to sell the property. An interest in the property may be held by a relative, who, on hearing that the property is going to be sold, makes a claim for his share of the proceeds. A family squabble may ensue which may be dragged out to interminable lengths, with you as the innocent bystander. There are other reasons why a seller sometimes "stalls" on delivering a deed. It has not infrequently happened that when a seller has your purchase contract in his possession, he acquires the daring and courage to attempt to sell the same piece of property at a higher price to someone else. If the second buyer is ready, the owner will "stall" in delivering the deed to you, hoping you will change your mind. Whenever possible, try to avoid a long lapse of time between your property purchase and the delivery of the deed.

(11) How Paid

The purchase contract should state definitely how the purchase price is to be paid, and where, especially if the seller takes either a first or second mortgage. In other words, if you bought the property without such terms being clearly stated, the seller might be in a position to "hold you up" on such terms as interest, amortization repayments, etc. It is particularly important in cases such as this, therefore, that the purchase contract include the amount of the proposed mortgage, the interest rate, the prepayment and amortizaion provisions—in fact all material terms of the mortgage which it is proposed to negotiate.

(12) Existing Mortgages

In the majority of country property transactions, especially those involving a house and land, you may find that there is an existing mortgage on the property. Therefore, if you buy either land, or land with a house, make sure that all the obligations of an existing mortgage held by the seller have been complied with. In all probability the lending institution which holds the *seller's* mortgage, will require that it be paid before he can sell the property to you. However, if *you* plan to assume the existing mortgage on a house and land, be sure to obtain from the *holder of the existing mortgage a statement in writing,* giving the amount of the unpaid mortgage, and the manner in which the balance is to be paid. If you don't take such precautions, you may find yourself with a larger unpaid mortgage than you realized, with unpaid interest, etc.

(13) Improvements Pending Deed Delivery

Often, especially when you buy land, you may want to make some change or improvements in the land even before you obtain the deed to the land. Some purchase contracts even provide for the buyer to take possession before obtaining the deed. This is a hazardous thing to do, and we *don't* recommend it. But if you *should* take possession before delivery of the deed, see to it that the purchase contract stipulates your *right* to make planned improvements, *and* your right to *remove* such improvements in the event the seller cannot furnish a clear title to the property. Otherwise you might forfeit your right to the improvements made, if the deed to the property were unavailable.

(14) Title Trickeries

As you know by this time, a good deal of trouble can arise where there is no clear title to property. It is important, therefore, that in the purchase contract the seller stipulates that title will be passed "free and clear of any encumbrances" except as specifically outlined in the contract. You should have your lawyer search the title and give you an "Abstract of Title." This "Abstract of Title" comprises a complete report of all the transactions of record through which the property has passed in known recorded history. Many titles in the country go back to Colonial times—to the original grants made by the Indians, either to the British Crown or the early settlers.

Title abstracts may be secured by any competent attorney. In addition there are, in some parts of the country, licensed title abstractors legally empowered to furnish such abstracts, such abstracts being recognized legally. In many areas you can have the title insured by a title guarantee insurance company. These latter companies issue policies that will protect you against such common inadequacies as may appear in the long history of the transfer of the property, and against defects and legal actions which may arise because of present unforeseen difficulties, such as wills, forgeries, divorce claims, etc. As in selecting your bank or lending institution, care should be exercised in choosing an established, conservative title insurance company.

Another protection which such a title search offers is the elimination of any questions as to the seller's right to sell the property to you, and your right to buy it. This title search carries the assurance for you, too, that the land or property you have *seen,* is the land or property you are *buying.* Furthermore, this title search will uncover any legal claims there may be against the property, such as judgments, liens, taxes, unpaid mortgages, assessments, and other possible charges. Your purchase contract should make it clear that in the event the seller cannot furnish a clear title to the property, the purchase contract shall become void, and any deposit or down payment shall be returned in full.

You can't be too careful about the title to your property. Your whole ownership may some day depend on its validity!

(15) Rents or Benefits

If you should buy country or farm property on which there are tenants paying rents, and you plan to retain such tenants for any period of time, the purchase contract should stipulate the definite dates on which first payments become payable to *you.*

(16) Place of Payment

Although this stipulation is not generally important, conditions have arisen on occasion where it has assumed importance. It is advisable, therefore, that the place of payment be designated in the terms of the purchase contract, and this should properly be a locality conveniently adjacent to the location of your property, often at the bank handling the mortgage.

We have now covered the principal items which should appear in the purchase contract. There may be other conditions necessitating the insertion of additional items. Your lawyer should be aware of these, and insert them accordingly. We would like to impress on you again the fact that the more complete your purchase contract is, the less chance there will be of future controversy.

(17) The Deed

Upon the fulfillment of the conditions outlined in the purchase contract, your payment of the amount agreed upon, and turning over the property under the conditions described in the contract, the seller of the property must deliver to you the "deed" to the property. A deed is a legal document which describes the property exactly, giving in detail all the items of ownership which pass from the seller to the buyer. A deed is not—and should not be—a simple thing. And that is another very good reason why you should be represented by a lawyer at this point in buying.

There are five principal requirements of a deed which a good lawyer will insist upon, and which it is necessary for you to understand.

(a) A deed should be in writing, phrased in proper legal terms. There is no room, in such an important document, for slipshod or ambiguous language. Your whole ownership may depend upon the wording of your deed.

(b) The deed should be made out in the name of

the *buyer*—yourself, or your wife if the property is to be recorded in her name, which isn't a bad idea, as this is the nearest thing you can get to incorporating yourself. In this way you can avoid personal responsibility in the event of a deficiency judgment action. We wish to impress on you again the importance of the deed's bearing the name of the actual owner, not any agent, nor representative, nor anyone else.

(c) The deed should contain a complete description of the property, based only on the survey, if you have one—which survey can become a part of the deed.

(d) The "consideration" of each party should be stated, practically repeating the terms of the purchase contract.

(e) The deed should be "signed, sealed, attested, acknowledged and delivered"—all mouth-filling legal phrases—but mighty important if certain questions should ever come up!

(18 & 19) Warranty and Quitclaim Deeds

There are two forms of deeds—*warranty* and *quitclaim* deeds. You should accept only a warranty deed. It is so called because the seller warrants or obligates himself, his agents, and/or his heirs, to defend your title to the property. The quitclaim deed, popular in the old West, where prospecting land was at stake, is a deed in which, as the name implies, the seller merely agrees to "quit" any claim he had on the property. But he doesn't obligate himself to defend the title to your property against anyone else who may have had a previous claim. In those days, you just shot it out. It should be pointed out, however, that even a warranty deed doesn't offer absolute protection. It is only as good as the person who makes it. There might be a claim against your property at some future time, and even though the former seller might in all honesty be willing to "defend" your title to the property, if he were "broke" at the time he wouldn't be able to finance a defense of the title. This discussion will serve to emphasize all the more clearly the advisability of providing yourself with a good survey and title insurance!

Deeds are sometimes subject to restrictions, either through definite clauses in the deed itself, or through municipal law. In other words, your right to unlimited and unrestricted use of the property can be curtailed by previous restrictions placed there by former owners, or added by municipal, village, or township statute. There are five types of property restriction with which you should be familiar.

(20) Zoning

One of these restrictions is zoning. You are probably familiar with the general operation of city zoning. This simply means that the city, village, or township authorities have by ordinance designated certain sections of the community for certain specific purposes only—residential, manufacturing, commercial, etc. The object of zoning is to make property values more or less stable, by assuring that localities will not change from one type to another, thus rapidly affecting values and investments. In the suburbs, by and large, zoning works to the advantage of the property owner. He is given some assurance that the locality in which he buys or builds a house will not turn rapidly into a business or manufacturing area.

If you should buy property in a *small* locality, try to ascertain whether zoning regulations are adhered to strictly. Zoning may or may not be enforced, depending on the locality. Zoning laws are so worded sometimes that it is comparatively easy to overturn them, if someone with influence or the "know-how" really wants to do so. The most satisfactory system of zoning is that in which interested property owners have the right to vote as to whether changes should be made in zoning laws.

On the other hand, some localities are so strictly zoned, that you may not be allowed to place your home where you want it, or run a business from your home. You also may be prevented from subdividing and selling off extra acres you may buy. A knowledge of zoning laws and prohibitions becomes an especially important consideration for those considering a productive homestead.

(21) Building Restrictions

Another of the property restrictions you should become familiar with is that of building restrictions. Many towns have them. Some specify the type of construction which may be used in certain areas. Others restrict the use of certain building materials. Where there are building codes, they are usually available at all city and town halls. Be sure you compare these codes with any plans you might have for the future building or development of your productive homestead. It might be better to avoid a locality having building codes which go beyond the essential requirements of safety in building and maintenance.

You may find, sometimes, that there are restrictions as to the width of roads and driveways that may be constructed within a township. The importance of looking closely into restrictions of this kind was impressed on the writer by the experience of a friend not so long ago. This family had bought three acres of land alongside a brook, about 60 feet from the road. Their property included what they accepted as a right-of-way to the road. There had never been any question as to their using it as a right-of-way in entering and leaving the property. When they filed plans for building their house, however, they discovered, to their consternation that the township building restrictions required that all rights-of-way or entrances to property off the street had to conform to a certain prescribed width. Their right-of-way fell two feet short of this requirement, and their application to build was denied. Under ordinary circumstances their investment would have been a total loss unless they were willing to acquire the additional two feet—which was, in fact, available but at an exorbitant price. Fortunately for them their purchase contract had stipulated that they were to receive a "marketable" deed on completing payments for the land. (They were buying the land on a regular monthly payment plan.) Because no one could build on the land with the right-of-way restriction, it was held that the seller could not have furnished a "marketable deed" and the money paid for the land was refunded in full. This story illustrates two points—the need for looking into all available zoning and building code ordinances, and the importance of securing a properly-worded purchase contract.

(22) Covenant Restrictions

There is another type of restriction called a covenant restriction. Covenants are agreements mutually entered into by any group of property owners in a certain section to accomplish certain ends to their common desires. Covenants are of many kinds, and may range from the type and cost of the building which you may erect, to the landscaping, architecture, and use to which you may put your property. As a rule you will find little of this type of restriction in the real country.

(23) Easements

You probably have heard of easements, but know them by their popular name of right-of-way. An easement in the legal sense is the right to use the land of another person without paying that person for the use of it. A right-of-way in the country may mean the right of neighbors to reach the road from an adjacent property, or a right-of-way from the road to reach a pasture, stream, woodlot, trail, or mountain, through your property. Many rights-of-way in the country date back a hundred years, and are still in effect. Sometimes they may have been all but forgotten, but lie in wait to trap a buyer not aware of them.

There is the story of Tom Woodward, who thought that a break in the stone wall separating him from the house next door was purely decorative. But not when he found that his neighbor was driving his cow night and morning across the place where Tom had planned his front lawn, and down to the stream which lay at the foot of Tom's property. Upon Tom's anguished howls, the neighbor hauled out an agreement over a century old providing for a "perpetual" right-of-way to the stream. The revival of the right-of-way through that particular spot was pure spite work but it had to be settled in court!

Or, the story of Olaf Anderson, whose property adjoined that of a neighbor whom Olaf liked. The driveway for the neighboring place was on Olaf's land, but when another family bought the place next to Olaf, and he took a dislike to them, he rolled a huge boulder right to the middle of the driveway. "How will we use the driveway, if you do that?" the newcomers asked. "You won't until you pay me four hundred dollars!" answered Olaf. They had bought a place without right-of-way.

So when you run across a little phrase on the deed which you are examining containing the words: "Subject to easements and covenants of record," you had better find out exactly what they are talking about—or else you might find that you have no real entrance to your land; that any of the villagers may traipse across your fields; that you may not be able to do any one of a hundred things!

When you have taken care of all the details briefly described in this chapter, and when you have arranged for the bond and mortgage, as described in full in our chapter on financing, you are ready for the final act in the drama of buying country property.

(24) The Closing

A closing is quite a dramatic affair. It generally takes place at the office of the lawyer for the seller; sometimes at the office of the lawyer for the buyer. From out of nowhere, apparently, a large number of people will have appeared—most of whom you have never seen before! It is carried off with all the formality of a wedding—which, after a manner of speaking, it is. You are going to be wedded to your property for better or worse, until death or the mortgage company do you part!

The seller is there with his lawyer and any members of his family who have an interest in the property. You are there with your lawyer, and probably your wife. There are other people whose identity you will probably never know. They sign mysterious papers; they whisper; they look rather suspiciously at you as if you were up to no good. The one individual, who represents the title guarantee insurance company, is always there to see that everything is right and proper.

The seller's lawyer and your own have had conferences, and have agreed on all the previous steps about which we have just spoken. The paid tax bills for the current year are presented, and any pro-rating of taxes is done now. Then you present a certified check, or maybe the actual cash for the amount you agreed to pay down on the property. In the meantime your lawyer has been reading the deed and he finds—or does not find—everything is as stated and agreed. The seller signs the deed, and gives it to your lawyer. It is witnessed, and with great pomp it is handed to you.

(25) Filing

Don't forget that you must file the final papers in the county clerk's office, or other office of record you have. Your ownership is not legally recognized until and unless you do such filing!

There is handshaking all around. The seller departs with your check safely tucked in his wallet. You pay your lawyer for his services (we hope) and are congratulated on being a pretty shrewd article and having acquired a treasure in the form of house and land. You and your wife depart, clutching to your hearts the precious deed, and leave the office for ill or good—the owners of a PIECE OF COUNTRY PROPERTY!